THE PROBLEM OF EVIL

Christian Concepts and the Book of Job

By

ALBION ROY KING

JOHN EDWARD JOHNSON PROFESSOR OF ETHICS AND RELIGION
CORNELL COLLEGE

87

THE RONALD PRESS COMPANY · NEW YORK

DEDICATION

To Saints Anonymous

who have achieved the mystery of suffering and religious faith.

I hold in memory the anonymous saint who first revealed to me this mystery. I cannot recover his name, and separation in time and space makes research difficult. It is little matter; he stands for a multitude, a choir invisible. I was a young minister in a village church. His sister, a mild little lady with a radiant face, stopped after church and asked me to call. I went with fear of pastoral duty: what could I who knew nothing of suffering say to one whose head had to be held in braces because a dread disease had wasted his spine? I have not forgotten his glowing face and cheerful faith. It was easy to return regularly on the receiving end of his ministration. He was the first to teach me the meaning of the words of Job from the King James Version:

Though he slay me, yet I will trust in him.

PREFACE

The problem of evil is the source of much that is truly great in religious thought and literature, perhaps because it is a problem with which every generation and every individual must struggle. It is a struggle that I began when, as a boy, I first encountered Bunyan's *Pilgrim's Progress*. From then until now the problem has been the central core of my studies. As a consequence, this is a book that had to be written, or at least a study that had to be completed as part of my own pilgrimage.

In the summer of 1932, after completing a doctoral dissertation at the University of Southern California on a pragmatic interpretation of the Book of Job, I was invited to lecture on that subject at the Pacific Palisades Summer Institute not far away. Each day the lecture was followed by a discussion period. An attentive but remarkably quiet listener was Dr. Alexander Hardie, a venerable and learned minister who kept close watch on the opinions of his younger brethren. At the end of the seminar he asked for the floor and addressed a few simple words of advice directly to me: "My dear scholarly young brother, if you will put those lectures away for fifteen years and then take them out you may know enough to talk about the Book of Job." Dr. Hardie belonged to a blunt-spoken generation; his dry remark was something of a shock, and a matter of some amusement to my contemporaries. But he was right and I know it even better after twenty years. I still know too little to interpret this document adequately. The Book of Job ought to be studied by every youth. Then it should be brought out for every succeeding crisis of life.

In this volume I have been concerned with the problem of evil as it confronts us of the twentieth century. The Job story and its philosophic ideas furnish the framework for the treatment. I have brought into this frame of reference ancient writings of the Middle East, the classical literature of tragedy, and Christian theology from St. Augustine to the present day. All biblical quotations are from the *Revised Standard* Version.

The ancient Hebrew view of man set him in the midst of a fearsome world. It is a simple cosmology nearly impossible for the twentieth century, and the basis of religion now has a tendency to shift to metaphysics, to a theory of the nature of reality. Central problems are the meaning of sin, the reasons for suffering and death, and the nature of destiny. I have tried to deal with these as the very real and acute problems they are for us today. It is my hope that this book will help others, troubled by the endless paradoxes and the shifting values of our contemporary life, to understand the essential nature of evil and to transcend it.

In preparing this book I have had in mind those readers for whom such an examination might prove exceptionally fruitful: first, the young ministers and teachers who have been my students and others like them who are seeking a guide for the understanding of the problem and its interpretation to this generation; secondly, college students of the humanities and the philosophy of religion, with whom much of this document has been wrought out in the college seminar on the literature of tragedy, and where it has met the test of the undergraduate classroom; and, generally, all thoughtful people who today need to attain perspective in looking at the evils of existence.

Readers will find here four positive suggestions for meeting squarely the implications of evil: survival after death, the intrinsic value of moral integrity, the disciplinary value of suffering, and the mystic experience of God which is made possible through suffering.

I am indebted to many individuals, including teachers, colleagues, and students, and especially the friends who have collaborated in the Cornell College extension seminars through the years. Two teachers call for particular mention: Dr. Elmer A. Leslie, of Boston University, who had my ear in his lectures on the Wisdom Literature at a time when I was doing graduate work in philosophy; and the late Dr. F. C. S. Schiller, of Oxford University, and the University of Southern California, who guided my research into the Book of Job; and whose influence is clearly discernible here. Three people have read the manuscript and given me much assistance. These are my wife, Fern Creekmore King; my colleague, Dr. Clyde Tull; and my brother, Karl C. King, Member of the House of Representatives from Pennsylvania. To President Russell D. Cole and the Trustees of Cornell College, I am grateful for the provision of the sabbatical leave which enabled me to complete this book. At Union Theological Seminary I found not only a fine library but a very able young Hebrew scholar, Dr. Samuel Terrien, with whom I enjoyed many profitable exchanges.

Mount Vernon, Iowa   ALBION ROY KING
    August, 1952

ACKNOWLEDGMENTS

I wish to express my appreciation to the publishers and authors who have granted me permission to use materials first appearing elsewhere. I am especially grateful to the Editorial Committee of the National Council of the Churches of Christ and Thomas Nelson & Sons for permission to quote from the *Revised Standard Version of the Holy Bible* published in 1952. I am also grateful for permission to quote the following: the poem "Wilderness," from *Cornhuskers* by Carl Sandburg, copyright 1918 by Henry Holt, Inc., copyright 1946 by Carl Sandburg; the sonnet "Eternity," reprinted from *Poems* by Irwin Edman, copyright 1925 by Simon and Schuster, Inc.; the poem "Dirge Without Music," from *The Buck in the Snow* by Edna St. Vincent Millay, copyright 1928 by Edna St. Vincent Millay; part of the James Rhoades translation "Of Patience Which is Perfect Joy," from *The Little Flowers of St. Francis*, The World's Classics, Oxford University Press, Inc., 1925. The chapter on "The Christian Devil" first appeared as an article in *Religion in Life*, Vol. XX, No. 1, and is reprinted here by agreement with the editors.

A. R. K.

CONTENTS

THE PROBLEM OF EVIL

Chapter 1

THE JOB STORY

An old man is sitting on an ash heap at the village dump, his eyes fixed in deep meditation. Presently he stirs to reach among the ashes for a piece of broken pottery. His skin needs attention, for he is covered from head to foot with loathsome boils. He is not a man of extreme age but well past the middle years, and when one's gaze overcomes the horror of the sight, one sees a person of dignity, reduced to desperation.

Once he was the proud and pious patriarch of the land of Uz whose name is Job. And he was very prosperous. He owned great herds of camels, oxen, and asses, a flock of seven thousand sheep, and his household was very great. He was the father of seven sons and three daughters, and each son was provided with a country home.

By the testimony of the omniscient Deity himself, Job was free of guile and straightforward in all his dealings with people. He feared God and turned away from evil. He was very scrupulous about the requirements of his religious cult. His sons held festive celebrations in the home of each in turn, and Job's fear of Yahweh led him, each time when the round was completed, to rise up early in the morning and offer sacrifices for their sanctification, lest any should have sinned or renounced God secretly.

In accordance with the orthodox ideas of the time, Job believed that there was a causal relation between his piety and his prosperity. Because of faithful service he was especially favored of the Almighty, and his affluence and respect among men were evidence of his integrity. Both in wealth and character he was greatest of all the sheikhs of the East.

Now look at Job's plight and wonder!

No one can better tell this story than those patient hands which have made our Bible, the ancient poets, scribes and monks who laboriously preserved the documents, modern scholars who have translated and interpreted the message, and the printers who have turned out the book for us. Here is the narrative part of the work with little embellishment.

A series of dire calamities, all in one day, fulfilled Job's premonitions of trouble. They happened when all the children were feasting together in the house of the eldest brother, perhaps a birthday celebration. A band of Sabean nomads drove off the oxen and the asses, even while some were plowing and others were feeding near by. Only one of the servants escaped to bring the news to Job. The second shock of bad news was the report of a lone surviving sheepherder that a bolt of lightning had destroyed the entire flock. Then came word that a marauding band of Chaldeans had driven off the camels and put to the sword all the slaves attending them except the one who escaped as messenger of ill tidings. Then the fourth and foulest blow came from the winds of heaven. A tornado struck the four corners of the eldest son's house and only one servant escaped alive from the holocaust.

Job's piety was sufficient to withstand this test. Fulfilling the forms of mourning, he arose and tore his outer garment from top to bottom, then shaved his head and fell down upon the earth in worship. His words were fervent and sincere:

> Naked I came from my mother's womb, and naked shall I return; the Lord gave, and the Lord has taken away; blessed be the name of the Lord. (1:21)[1]

[1] All quotations from the Bible are from the *Revised Standard Version*, by special permission of the publishers, Thomas Nelson & Sons, Inc., as stated elsewhere. This most recent revision goes back to the pattern of the King James Version by translating the Hebrew word "Yahweh" as "the Lord." Very properly the translators have rejected the misspelled word "Jehovah." Throughout the text of this work we shall follow the practice of using the word "Yahweh" for the Hebrew God as it appears in the original text.

In no mite did he yield to the common human proclivity for cynical acts of sin or make a foolish charge against the Almighty.

But this was not the end of his suffering. Shortly a foul hand was laid against his own skin. He was smitten with a disease of boils from the sole of his foot to the crown of his head, and in the deepest grip of mourning and mystery he went out of the house to sit among the ash heaps.

The dramatic writer of our story has insight into supernatural causes of these calamities. Twice he pulls back the curtain upon the councils of heaven when the sons of God come to present themselves before Yahweh. Among them is The Satan,[2] a restless spirit who passes to and fro upon the earth in search of disinterested and honest piety.

Yahweh issues a challenge to Satan concerning his favorite: "Have you considered my servant Job, that there is none like him on the earth, a blameless and upright man, who fears God and turns away from evil?"

But Satan is skeptical. "Does Job fear God for nought?" The Almighty has supplied him with all blessings and surrounded him with every protection. 'But put forth thy hand now, and touch all that he has, and he will curse thee to thy face." Satan supposes that he understands human nature. But permission granted for the testing, and the first series of disasters accomplished, Job remains steadfast, a refutation of Satanic cynicism.

Then a second scene in heaven brings Satan again among the sons of God in council to make report. And again Yahweh challenges the satirical spirit with his boast about his favorite: "Have you considered my servant Job . . . ? He still holds fast his integrity, although you moved me against

[2] In the Hebrew language, "The Satan" is the title given this spirit, and it is so translated in some of the modern versions of the Bible. From here on we shall follow the tradition of the King James Version and drop the definite article. What had originally been a title became a proper name. See Chapter 4.

him, to destroy him without cause." But no evidence can satiate Satan's cynicism. "Skin for skin! All that a man has he will give for his life. But put forth thy hand now, and touch his bone and his flesh, and he will curse thee to thy face."

With divine permission then, Satan strikes the person of Job. It is a foul blow and there he sits among the ashes, caught in cogitation of the deepest and darkest mystery of life.

Now his wife turns against him. In ancient times a man could not lay his troubles on his wife. She is not that important. He alone is responsible for the conduct of his affairs. But she is the symbol of final rejection by his community. Social attitudes toward suffering are a part of the problem of evil.

After all this, can Job still hang on to the idea that he is a good man, favored of the Almighty? Isn't it time to curse God and die? But still he is the saint who does not sin with his lips. He rebukes his spouse in what is by now a half-convincing platitude: "You speak as one of the foolish women would speak. Shall we receive good at the hand of God and shall we not receive evil?" He takes a firm grip on the broken piece of jar with which he tends his boils, a sort of masochistic instrument, and subsides into a long, dark silence.

Three neighboring sheikhs of equal social standing, fellow searchers after divine wisdom and devotees of the poetic muse, hear of the plight of their friend. Eliphaz the Temanite, Bildad the Shuhite, and Zophar the Naamathite make an appointment together and come to bemoan and comfort him. As they draw near and look from a distance they are unable to recognize Job, so great is his affliction, and they lift up their voices in weeping. Then each man rends his robe and, casting dust in the air above his head, magical protection against such an evil demon, he cautiously approaches to sit down beside Job among the ashes. So they remain for seven days and seven nights, no one speaking a word.

After the long vigil, Job opens his mouth and breaks the
silence in the bitterest wail ever recorded from human lips.
In strident poetic cadences he curses the day of his birth.

> Let the day perish wherein I was born,
>   and the night which said,
>   "A man-child is conceived."
> Let that day be darkness!
>   May God above not seek it,
>   or light shine upon it. (3:3-4)

For twelve verses the curse continues with increasing bitterness, and then for seven more he bewails the fate which
brought him forth from Sheol, that abode beyond, where the
soul comes from and whither it goes. And finally he re-
nounces life and longs for death, welcome release from the
travail and fears that have gotten hold of him.

Eliphaz the Temanite shakes the dust out of his robe and
moves with dignity and gentle courtesy to the poetic communion of souls. He opens by reminding Job of days before,
when he had held the role of instructor and upholder of the
ways of God to man. Now that the role has been shifted,

> Is not your fear of God your confidence,
>   and the integrity of your ways your hope? (4:6)

This is the introduction for a forceful poetic statement of
the ancient Hebrew orthodoxy, the doctrine that God rules
the universe in evenhanded justice, and that the sufferings
which befall the lot of human kind are retribution for sin.
Foolish is the man who thinks, because of temporary prosperity, that he is especially favored and can therefore begin to
tamper with the principles of righteousness. Man must always remember that he is a creature and that God rules the
universe.

As an item of revelation, presented to him in a night vision, Eliphaz cautiously approaches the profound mystery of
man's finiteness and God's infinity. With all his aspiration

for perfection, no man can be just before his Maker. A gulf yawns between the creature, even the angels, and the Creator. Happy is the man, therefore, whom God correcteth. Man should never despise the chastening of the Almighty. It is the way of instruction for the wise in the principles of right living.

But Job is unmoved by this approach. The long silence had an ominous import, even an eloquent aspect of accusation. The rending of garments and throwing of dust in the air were not sympathy pure and simple; they had the magical purpose of warding off evil contamination from the would-be comforters. Now the sermon of Eliphaz, with all its flattering references to past glories makes the none too subtle inference that all is well with the universe and even with Job himself if he will but cling to the spirit of the pious platitudes of the prose prologue.

Job does not rise to the bait of conciliation, for it would imply a personal guilt which he does not feel. His response continues and deepens in bitterness. One who is ready to faint has a right to expect kindness from his friends, even though he should forsake the fear of the Almighty under stress. But this Job has not done. Indeed, his fear of the Almighty, plus his fearless and thoughtful searching of his own heart, furnishes the conflict with that traditional theory of divine justice which is the problem of the debate.

Job calls for evidence of his guilt. Let reproof be of deeds, not of words. There can be no reproof of words spoken in desperation, only understanding and sympathy. The seventh chapter of the symposium is one of the most poignant poetic statements of the dark and hopeless plight of human existence. There is a warfare to man upon earth. His days are spent in such labor that he longs for the night and then he lies down to such troubled dreams that he longs for the day. And his days are swifter than a weaver's shuttle, and there is no hope in them. Is it all a testing? Then

What do I to thee, thou watcher of men? (7:20)

Eliphaz has offered Job the easy way of submission. He need not acknowledge some specific sin but simply agree that his afflictions are the result of the general sinfulness of men. There is no perfection. We are all caught in the same condemnation.

Job's refusal to take this course furnishes the three friends with their problem. It is simply incomprehensible to them. Their theology is involved in their sense of security. A subtle psychological need supports the comfortable person in such a belief. His prosperity confirms his ego in its natural confidence of rightness with the universe. If God rewards the good man with prosperity and punishes the sinner with want and illness, then this prosperity is his assurance and ground of security. Spontaneous thought pursues the same pattern, even if one's god is nature or fate or economic laws. If misfortune can befall Job for no reason at all, the friends are not secure either. Job must be wicked or else the sun of faith fades out of their sky. When their creed is threatened, wise men come to its defense, often though it means a pitiless attitude toward a friend.

Job has suggested that the speeches of one who is desperate are as wind, and Bildad the Shuhite takes him up, with a doubtful compliment that his words are like a mighty wind. Then he goes on to argue more directly and positively than Eliphaz that the justice of the Almighty cannot be perverted. Both the wisdom of the fathers and the operations of nature should teach him that retribution follows sin as surely as withered grass and parched water reeds follow a dry season. He makes the direct charge that the death of Job's children was punishment for their sins, and takes no pains to disguise a similar inference about Job's afflictions.

Job ignores the insult to his children and the direct attack upon himself. He is preoccupied with a soliloquy on the dark mystery of life, set off by the revelation of Eliphaz that a gulf yawns between man and the righteousness of God. How can man be just with one who is the sum of all wisdom? And how can he contend with the mighty power which removes mountains and shakes the earth and commands the sun and stretches out the heavens and creates the constellations and treads upon the waves of the sea? In such a thoughtful contemplation of providence, Job falls into a mood of wonder and is almost ready to repent, but then he turns to consider his own plight, and his heart again fills with bitterness at the injustice of life:

> I am blameless; I regard not myself;
>   I loathe my life.
> It is all one; therefore I say,
>   he destroys both the blameless and the wicked.
> When disaster brings sudden death,
>   he mocks at the calamity of the innocent.
> The earth is given into the hand of the wicked;
>   he covers the faces of its judges—
>   if it is not he, who then is it? (9:21-24)

A more direct challenge to the goodness of God could scarcely be imagined. Yet Job subsides into a more plaintive mood as he bewails the remoteness and impersonality of God so that the two cannot come together in judgment.

> There is no umpire between us,
>   who might lay his hand upon us both. (9:33)

Then he cries out for mercy from both God and man and again bemoans the fate that brought him into the world. In the anticipation of imminent death, and passage to the land of darkness from whence there shall be no returning, he concludes.

All this draws the scorching fire of Zophar the Naamathite. To his other evident guilt Job has now added the sin of blasphemy, and God has exacted less than he deserves. Zophar ridicules the presumption of Job in putting puny reason against revealed truth. The secrets of God are hidden even from wisdom. He promises restoration of all his affluence for mere submission, and he lodges a dire threat for continued obstinance. In this theology the first demand on Job for his reinstatement in the good grace of both man and God is an admission of guilt.

Job takes up the challenge that divine truth is beyond reason, known only to wise old men by revelation. The orthodox notion that all suffering is retribution arises not from revelation but from the subtle psychological factors which lead those who are at ease to have contempt for misfortune. If we examine actual experience, we see that God deals in an omnipotent and despotic way with all creatures, not only with men but with animals as well, indifferent to the sin of individuals.

There is no gain from a dishonest facing of these facts. If the Almighty has to be defended with lies, then his advocates are physicians of no value. He asks them to hold their peace while he faces this thing out with God. He may be slain for it, but he will maintain the integrity of his ways, and he turns to address the Deity, assured that there is an inner approach to him open only to the man of integrity. His salvation lies in a negative fact that no godless man shall come before him. So he pleads his innocence, crying out for a fair hearing, and falls into a piercing description of human woe.

The verses that follow in the fourteenth chapter have matched the mood of man in facing death for thousands of years.

> Man that is born of a woman
>> is of few days, and full of trouble.
> He comes forth like a flower, and withers;
>> he flees like a shadow, and continues not. (14:1-2)

God ought to allow man to live his brief span in peace, for when it is over, that is the end. A tree cut down may sprout again; not man.

> But man dies, and is laid low;
>   man breathes his last, and where is he?
> As waters fail from a lake,
>   and a river wastes away and dries up,
> So man lies down and rises not again;
>   till the heavens are no more he will not awake,
>   or be roused out of his sleep. (14:10-12)

If only God would hide him in Sheol for a time and then revive him after his anger has subsided.

> If a man die, shall he live again? (14:14)

He toys with a great idea, but as yet the hope of it does not take firm hold of his heart.

Twice round the circle they go. With rising vehemence and sharpening thrust the three wise ones defend the justice of the Almighty, and, with a victim before them as a horrible example, they paint in lurid pictures the fate of the wicked. There is no progress in their argument from this point on, only repetition. A third round of speeches is started but not finished. In it Eliphaz comes to the final break with his friend by openly charging him with a specific list of sins, injustice to the weak and lack of charity to the poor, sins the ancient Hebrew prophets charged against the rulers of their day.

Bildad makes a feeble final effort, but Zophar remains silent. They fail to subdue and harness the "wild ass's colt" to their theology. But it is an impressive doctrine they have expounded. It is the faith that the universe operates in accordance with an absolute moral order. This was a lofty and inspiring theology when it was expounded in the oracles of the early prophets who cried out against the wickedness of kings and explained the political reverses of Israel as punishment for the social evils fostered by the ruling classes. Now, in the face of sufferings like Job's, the teaching sounds hollow and perverse. Will the faith of man in the unity of the moral order and the natural order stand up under the strain of such personal experience?

This is the philosophical problem with which the poet who first penned these verses was struggling. But he also has a deeper religious question. What is the place of religion in man's experience? Must man's devotion to God and the cultivation of all those experiences called religious be purchased by the guarantee of prosperity and happiness? Is Satan's slur against human nature justified by the performance of man before God? Is there an experience of faith which has a supreme value above all other experience, good or bad?

Job responds to each speech in turn, paying less and less attention to what the friends level at him. He has heard all such chatter before. He longs for an end to "windy words" or a reversal of the roles that would let him take the part of the comforter. He turns his attention to God and his speeches are addressed to the ages. Alternating between moods of bitter complaint at the injustice of existence, wistful hope, and black despair, he achieves a scant comfort from the thought that soon death will end his suffering and he will be hidden away in the underworld.

There is a progression of thoughtful exploration in these Job speeches toward a series of climaxes. The first is a flash of insight coming toward the close of the nineteenth chapter after several stanzas in which he dips very low into the cup of human woe. It is the confidence that his moral vindication must be sure, and even though death intervenes, the vindicator will bring him up to face God above the ground. This word is so sure that it must be written in a book or engraved on the rock for all to see forever.

Then in the twenty-third chapter, Job rises to the certainty that God must be a reasonable being if he just knew where he could find him. Should he ever have a chance to stand up before the Almighty to plead his cause, he would fill his mouth with arguments. At the moment the chance escapes him, for God eludes his search, both before and behind, to the left and on the right hand. But this anticipates events to come.

Amid much confusion in the argument, caused, perhaps, by the inclusion of extraneous poems and the probable disarrangement of some of the stanzas, the friends subside and Job makes an end of this poetic symposium in a long monologue which summarizes his experience and problem. In a poem of fine dramatic power, he reviews the glories of his former life, contrasting these with the miseries that have descended upon him. Because God has forsaken him, even the children of men who formerly were objects of his charity now hold him in derision. He comes to a high emotional climax in a series of poetic oaths which maintain his moral integrity and deny his guilt of the sins listed in Eliphaz' indictment. It is an important catalogue of the virtues expected of the good man in ancient Judea.

As Job and his erstwhile comforters subside into a brooding silence, with no decision drawn in the debate, a new character enters the stage of action. For some time he has been listening silently in the background, greatly shocked at the fearless manner in which Job has challenged the character of God and attacked the commonly accepted dogma that all suffering is retribution for sin. He is equally incensed at the three friends because they have so miserably failed to justify God and convince Job of his error.

Elihu is a young man, a student of theology devoted to the cultivation of wisdom. And because of his youth and his respect for age, he has held his peace for so long.

> I said, "Let days speak,
>   and many years teach wisdom."
> But it is the spirit in a man,
>   the breath of the Almighty,
>   that makes him understand. (32:7-8)

His modesty does not trouble him long when once he gets under way. He is full of words and ready to burst, like the new wineskins.

> Bear with me a little, and I will show you,
>   for I have yet something to say on God's behalf.
> I will fetch my knowledge from afar,
>   and ascribe righteousness to my Maker.
> For truly my words are not false;
>   one who is perfect in knowledge is with you. (36:2-4)

But he does not fulfil the promise of such an introduction. For the most part he gives us, with much arrogance, a tiresome repetition of the arguments already exhausted by the three orthodox friends. God is perfect wisdom. He can do no wrong. Suffering is an exact retribution for sin, but it also has the purpose of instructing and disciplining man. Job and the friends alike have been guilty of the sin of pride. Job's rebellion is blasphemous and sure to bring dire retribution.

Inferior poems though they may be, the words of Elihu serve a dramatic purpose in the narrative, for a storm seems to be gathering on the distant horizon. Elihu begins to draw illustrations of divine majesty and mystery from the gathering of the thick storm cloud, the flash of lightning on the sand dunes and the roll of thunder across the heavens. In the theatrical production of the Book of Job by Stuart Walker, Eliphaz fingers his beard in that direction, and as the wind blows through his whiskers, he makes a hasty exit. Bildad gathers up his tattered robe and runs for protection. Zophar suddenly remembers his unprotected flocks on the hillside and flies to their relief. As the storm approaches nearer, Elihu becomes nervous and somewhat faltering in speech, and just as it breaks upon the scene he runs for shelter. Job alone is left among the ashes, the fury of the storm matching the turmoil of his soul, as he falls on his face awaiting the final blow of death.

Then a wondrous thing happens. Job has all the time

longed for his chance to face the Almighty in person. The
black mood of despair gradually gives way toward the end of
the speeches as vague anticipation grips his heart. But the
manifestation of Yahweh comes with dramatic surprise.
Nature, the same indifferent mass against which the desert
shiekh must struggle to win a living from the wilderness, even
the same ferocious power which smote the house of his son
and destroyed his children, now becomes Job's pathway to
God. For out of the whirlwind comes the voice of Yahweh
speaking directly to him, inviting him to the verbal contest
he has so long demanded.

> Gird up your loins like a man,
>   I will question you, and you shall declare to me.
> Where were you when I laid the foundation of the earth?
>   Tell me, if you have understanding.
> Who determined its measurements—surely you know!
>   Or who stretched the line upon it?
> On what were its bases sunk,
>   or who laid its cornerstone,
> when the morning stars sang together,
>   and all the sons of God shouted for joy? (38:3-7)

Job lifts an eye and ear from his ashy bed, all attention, but
opens not his mouth. Yahweh speaks in lofty poetic cadences,
oracles worthy of the dignity of a theophany. Yet whatever
our theory of divine inspiration, we must find in these stanzas
a wisdom in human vessels; otherwise we must suffer keen
disappointment that there is no answer to Job's problem, no
direct attention paid to the basic questions of the debate.
But no word of the poet in the final reach of his insight confirms the orthodox doctrine of Eliphaz and his comrades.

These are nature poems in the highest order of beauty.
A series of rhetorical questions demands how much mortal
man knows or can know about the origin and purpose and
the inner working of the universe. The outer frame of the
cosmos is reviewed, and then Yahweh turns to the mysteries
of the living species which inhabit it.

Job is subdued. He was going to stand up to such an opportunity and fill his mouth with arguments, but now the impulse fails him.

> Behold, I am of small account; what shall I answer thee?
>   I lay my hand on my mouth.
> I have spoken once, and I will not answer;
>   twice, but I will proceed no further. (40:4-5)

The climax of this theophany comes in two awe-inspiring poems describing Behemoth and Leviathan, hippopotamus and crocodile, two mysterious creatures which connect the world of the living with that mythical realm of Semitic antiquity in which a chaotic monster, Tiamat, with a brood of such fearsome creatures, has a hand in creation itself.

The basic insight here is that an order and purpose exists in the world, but it is hidden in cosmological mystery. Man must lay hold upon it by faith. And this is the outcome for Job.

> I know that thou canst do all things,
>   and that no purpose of thine can be thwarted.
>
>   *   *   *   *   *
>
> I had heard of thee by the hearing of the ear,
>   but now my eye sees thee;
> therefore I despise myself,
>   and repent in dust and ashes. (42:2, 5-6)

He who had known no sense of guilt concerning the common faults of social living, who was proclaimed by Yahweh as a shining example of upright and straightforward character, now confronted by God in the midst of the mysterious struggle of life, is humble at last. In the mood of confession he finds peace. Shalom!

This narrative ends, as it began, in a prose epilogue. The palm of victory in the debate is delivered to Job. Eliphaz, Bildad and Zophar are commanded to offer sacrifices to expiate their failure, and Job is bidden to pray for them. Then Yahweh turns the tables for Job and restores his prosperity so that his latter end is blest above the beginning, both in possessions and children. His three new daughters, Jemimah, Keziah, and Keren, are the fairest women of the land.

Chapter 2

UNRAVELING THE BOOK

As you have read our Job story in Chapter 1, have you by chance or design followed the text of the book in the Bible? If so, you have doubtless wondered where one can find the thread of thought and action set forth. Amid all the fullness of vivid poetic imagery and the complicated skein of argument, how can such a narrative be unwound? Before going further, the book should be read through, if possible at one sitting.

The Book of Job is not an easy pattern to unravel. Many difficult questions cluster about it, and we could not get far except for the long and painstaking labors of scholars whose linguistic and historical knowledge has opened the work to modern readers.

The profound penetration of the Job philosophy into the deepest mysteries of human existence, and the exquisite beauty of its literary flowering, have never failed to impress the thoughtful reader; yet the book remains for the majority of people a hidden work. Popular reading which now seldom gets beyond the prose narrative of the first two chapters will certainly go deeper as the work is retranslated and expounded in the future. Much of its imagery and many aphorisms are common parlance, but few have traced their meanings to the source. Literary critics of the past have with one voice proclaimed the Book of Job among the greatest masterpieces of any time or language. As its message is unfolded to us in the work of more recent scholars, its value in no way diminishes. And for our troubled times it takes on added interest.

The purpose of this chapter is to review and choose from the scholarly opinions on some of these enigmatic questions what seems to be the most intelligent position from which to expound the philosophical implications of the book. Since this is not a commentary, it will not be necessary to resolve all problems or to trace all scholarly opinions.

Place in Literature

The Book of Job stands unique and alone, both in the Bible and in the world's literature a lofty and austere peak rising from a fertile plain. It has elements of the epic; yet Job is no epic hero like Odysseus or Aeneas. The suffering aspects of human experience are dramatically portrayed. A Sophocles might have turned it into tragic drama, as some modern interpreters have tried to do; yet the work itself is neither a drama designed for the theater nor a tragedy in the Greek sense. The tragic hero of Greek literature is caught in a web of heroism, passion, and causes hidden from him by the nature of things so that he confronts inevitable doom from which there is no escape and no ultimate solution or meaning. Such is the case of Oedipus, Antigone, Electra, and Orestes. Aeschylus may have extricated Prometheus from his sufferings, but the story is lost, and in any case Prometheus was a god, not a human being. The unmerited sufferings of Job have a tragic aspect, as that word is often used, but they are not tragedy in this technical sense because the problem is not left without solution in the book, even though the discernment of that solution may be difficult.

There is no obscurity about the statement of the problem itself. Job on the ash heap and the friends tossing dust in the air, Job's bitter complaint, the orthodox accusations against him, and his declaration of moral integrity, these are vivid enough. But the very problematic and obscure nature of the solutions suggested and pursued in the book makes it a rich treasure to be mined repeatedly by the human spirit. After all, it is evident that there are no easy solutions to this problem.

This book was first discovered by the author as an adolescent when death touched the country home and the somber mood of the poem matched the mysterious reverence of the family circle. Then it was read aloud at the bedside of his mother when she knew and all knew that she had only weeks to live. Repeatedly, in the evil times which have overtaken the world, and always after dipping into some segment of the voluminous literature of the scholars who have opened the ancient document to modern readers, the author has reread it, never without discovery of some new insight upon the most difficult problems of human existence.

The subject is man and God, that ellipse with two foci which is religion. At one focus is man in all his finiteness and struggle for the good life, and then the focus abruptly shifts to God, designer, creator, ruler of the cosmos—and in the transition lies all the enigmatic questions about man's relation to God and the universe.

Traditionally, Job is listed among the wisdom books. These include Proverbs and Ecclesiastes in the Bible and The Wisdom of Solomon and Ecclesiasticus in the Apocrypha. Job is the only one of these, however, which carries a single theme throughout, and both in poetic power and philosophic insight it attains a level far above the didactic wisdom of these other works. The same may be said for the comparison with the wisdom literature of Egypt and Mesopotamia.

The author of Job also had an incredible store of learning. All the wisdom and science of ancient Egypt and Babylonia contributed to his work. He was master of Semitic cosmology and nature lore, as well as of the moral and religious insights of the Hebrew sages. Comparisons with other world literature usually call up the names of Homer, Virgil, Dante, Milton, and Goethe. But Dante's *Commedia* alone bears an equal position at the pinnacle of masterpieces of religious thought and art. Of these two works, Emil Kraeling has said:

> [The Book of Job] remains one of the greatest books of all time, the noblest product of the pre-Christian religious life, as the *Commedia* is the most excellent poetic offspring of Christian piety. Together they are the morning and the evening star of the sky of religious literature.[1]

Many of the passages of Job can be read as separate poems. There are elegies, doxologies and hymns to the attributes and works of deity, laments, prayers, and desperate appeals both to friends and to God. For full appreciation the reader needs to be warned by what Richard Moulton, in his *Literary Study of the Bible*,[2] called "the rhetoric of antiquity which was the delight in speech for its own sake." When the poet sets off on an idea, he does not drive relentlessly to its unfolding logic after the manner of philosophical literature. The Hebrew verse is a parallel couplet, or rarely a triplet, in which the second or third lines repeat the thought of the first with a change in the metaphor, and from there the idea is carried through every conceivable simile, sometimes for many verses, thus greatly enriching the imagery. But the progression is slow. The dialogue is not a series of sharp exchanges, like the modern drama, but a round of long addresses. While Job surely was not intended for theatrical production, yet, like most other ancient poetry, it was designed for oral presentation, and even in translation it must be read aloud to produce the mood which is so essential to its message.[3]

[1] Emil G. Kraeling, *The Book of the Ways of God* (New York: Chas. Scribner's Sons, 1939), p. 8.

[2] (Boston: D. C. Heath & Co., 1895), p. 40.

[3] Horace M. Kallen undertook in his *The Book of Job as a Greek Tragedy* (New York: Dodd, Mead & Co., 1918) to reconstruct the text after the pattern of Euripidean tragedy. It is said to have had several stage presentations. Without radical adaptation, however, it fits the pattern neither in form nor in meaning. The writer once attended a theatrical performance of the Book of Job from the text of the King James Version, unchanged. Produced by Stewart Walker, with George Sommes taking the part of Job, it ran for several weeks in New York, Boston, and Philadelphia.

Let the following be read as a fine example. It is an integral part of Job's speeches, yet it can stand alone:

> Has not man a hard service upon earth,
>   and are not his days like the days of a hireling?
> Like a slave who longs for the shadow,
>   and like a hireling who looks for his wages,
> so I am allotted months of emptiness,
>   and nights of misery are apportioned to me.
> When I lie down I say, "When shall I arise?"
>   But the night is long,
>   and I am full of tossing till the dawn.
> My flesh is clothed with worms and dirt;
>   my skin hardens, then breaks out afresh.
> My days are swifter than a weaver's shuttle,
>   and come to their end without hope.
> Remember that my life is a breath;
>   my eye will never again see good.
> The eye of him who sees me will behold me no more;
>   while thy eyes are upon me, I shall be gone.
> As the cloud fades and vanishes,
>   so he who goes down to Sheol does not come up;
> he returns no more to his house,
>   nor does his place know him any more. (7:1-10)

Place in Bible History

The original Book of Job, we are told by Hebrew scholars, is the richest outpouring of the Hebrew language, and yet it is unlike any other document in the Hebrew Bible. It is a dialect of Hebrew and with a vocabulary partly peculiar to itself. Except for a single allusion to the river Jordan, there is no reference in the book to any place in Palestine or to any event in Hebrew history. No characteristic practice of Jewish piety, or ritual, or any religious idea peculiar to Judaism is expounded in the work. One of the most cherished doctrines, fostered by the great prophets, that suffering is retribution for sin, is subjected to severe criticism and modification.

The work might even be the product of a foreign hand, Edomite, for instance, as has been suggested.[4] Uz may be located in that direction, according to one theory based on modern archeological excavations, although no one has ever identified the place for certain. Job is described as greatest of the "children of the East," and his three friends were probably sheikhs of the borders of Arabia. Wisdom was an international pursuit, the children of Israel having no monopoly on literature.

But all this does not add up to foreign authorship. The Job poem is Hebrew in language, it is in the Hebrew Bible, and it has had from the beginning an influential place in the formative history of Judaism. And there is no literature of the Edomites available for comparison. If the author belonged there, then his work has been thoroughly naturalized in Judah. And now it is the treasured possession of all humanity.

The time and place of Job in Old Testament history are also hard to fix. There are no positive historical clues. Most of the other documents can be arranged in a progression and many of them can be dated. Then we must speculate as to where the particular ideas developed in Job and where the language employed belong in this progression. This is precarious reasoning. Not only is the progression problematic but the assumption must be made that conflicting strains of doctrine, or differing stages of maturity in their development, would not likely occur at the same time. Yet there are clues of this sort which may not only help us to find a probable date for Job, but in following them we may come to a better understanding of the work itself.

Job might have been written as early as the time of the prophet Jeremiah, about 600 B.C., who shares some of the sad experience of life, and the questioning attitude toward it,

[4] Robert H. Pfeiffer, *Introduction to the Old Testament* (New York: Harper & Bros., 1941), pp. 675-83, holds this view.

which we find in Job. Yet our poem has a maturity in the
discussion which hardly belongs to the prophetic era, unless,
perchance, it were the work of foreign hands who were not
living in the same intellectual realm as the prophets.

Our poetic philosopher belongs in a time when Jewish
thought had achieved an advanced theological position, when
God was thought of both as ruler of nations and the cosmos,
and as a God of absolute justice. When he wrote, the individual had emerged as the center of religious interest, and the
pursuit of personal righteousness had become the ideal goal
of life. This had not always been the case in Hebrew history,
it would seem. The book was probably written before the
idea of resurrection had become a commonly accepted doctrine in Judah, since the concept is so specifically denied in
the words of Job and never affirmed by his opponents in the
argument. In the disputed passage, 19:25-27 (to be discussed
in Chapter 7), we may have the earliest literary suggestion
of a possible resurrection.

A time after the return of the Jews from exile, probably
in the fourth century B.C. and before the end of the Persian
era, seems to fit this requirement. But let us trace more completely this line of speculation.

Prophetic Theology

Early Hebrew thought of deity is little above the level of
primitive polytheism. Yahweh is God of the tribe and he is
sole deity only for members of the nation. His dealings are
quite arbitrary, sometimes on the level of magical propitiations. Abraham argues with Yahweh under the oaks of
Mamre that the Judge of all the earth should do right in his
dealings with Sodom (Gen. 18).

The prophets were the architects of Israel's mature theology, both in its monotheism and in its absoluteness, both in
making Yahweh ruler of nature and nations and in proclaim-

ing his absolute justice in dealing with men. But these concepts were not established by a sudden revelation. In the
eighth century they thundered the pronouncement of doom
upon the kingdoms because the leaders rejected justice, and
they promised rescue for the remnant which would turn
about and deal justly with the people. The preachment had
to stand the test of history. The dogma of absolute power
and absolute justice combined in Yahweh was hardly secured
firmly until after the exile and then it had to face serious
doubts.

The terrible calamities of war and captivity, so graphically
portrayed in the poems of Lamentations 2 and 4, focused the
problem of evil at a different angle. No longer is the question,
"Why is the favored nation so unrighteous?" but, "Why do
the chosen people suffer?" These two questions the problem
of moral evil and the problem of suffering, rise up in history
to confront every cult of religion and every system of philosophy.

After the exile, the Elders of Judah, too busy for theology,
set about the difficult tasks of rebuilding the Temple and the
city walls, establishing the law, and organizing communal life.
Visions of a new Jerusalem, a purified worship, and a more
glorious Temple as the heart of the community inspired the
oracles of Haggai and Zechariah and the statesmanship of
Ezra and Nehemiah. But the question of divine justice must
have been both persistent and difficult. Why worship a God
unable to save his chosen nation from captivity? The message of the older prophets surely sounded vacant and hollow
now. A strange sort of divine justice which punishes Israel
for idolatry and unrighteousness by subjugation to an empire
which was the mother of idolatry and the epitome of tyranny!

There was skepticism, but in spite of it the word of the
prophets prevailed and the absolute justice of God became
a dogma.

Then it was the prophetic message and the circumstances
of the exile which established also the absoluteness of the
God Yahweh as ruler of the cosmos and the disposer of na-
tions. We find the doctrine first in those chapters of the
Book of Isaiah (40-55) which are assigned to Second Isaiah.
Here is a sample:

> Thus says God, the LORD,
>> who created the heavens and stretched them out,
>> who spread forth the earth and what comes from it,
> who gives breath to the people upon it,
>> and spirit to those who walk in it:
> "I am the LORD, I have called you in righteousness,
>> I have taken you by the hand and kept you;
> I have given you as a covenant to the people,
>> a light to the nations,
>> to open the eyes that are blind,
> to bring out the prisoners from the dungeon,
>> from the prison those who sit in darkness. (Isa. 42:5-7)

If the Job poem was written earlier, we might say that this
writer had depended on it. But Job is so much superior, both
in conception and in literary force. Both writers were independent artists, and both undoubtedly had sources of international wisdom and cosmology which are now lost to us.
Both writers state the dogma of God's absoluteness and justice, but in the time of the Job composition it was so well
established in popular thought that the author found it necessary to raise sharp questions about it.

The Second Isaiah is also the first Biblical writer to offer
an answer to the troublesome doubt about why the righteous
suffer. In a beautiful series of poems (42:1-4; 49:1-6; 50:4-9;
52:13-53:12) he extols the "Servant of Yahweh" for his sufferings because they are vicarious, and through them the
redemption of man is accomplished. From the first, this
Servant must have been identified with the nation, although
later the vicarious suffering doctrine was given an individual

application to the trials of great heroes, like Jeremiah or the predicted Messiah. New Testament thought takes these poems to heart as explanation for the sufferings of the Christ.

But the Job philosopher seems never to have thought of the idea, or to have found it meaningless as applied to the man of Uz. Job does not suffer as a result of some public service, but rather he is the victim of demonic aspects of what we might term "nature." This complicates the problem—for us at least, for nature is a modern concept. And "demons"! How do they fit into the scheme?

There are affinities between Job and Second Isaiah, but their relation in time cannot be fixed with finality. Christian piety may superficially think of the oracles in Isaiah as much advanced in religious concept but the Job debates penetrate much deeper into this problem. Even that would not determine the age of either. But the more probable succession seems to be that Job struggles with religious dogmas which the prophet of the exile had helped to fix in Jewish thought through a century or more of time preceding.[5]

Suffering and the Individual

The sages and wise men of the Semitic world were always interested in the individual. In Egypt and Babylonia they were moralizers and inventors or collectors of folk wisdom designed to keep the nobles noble and the rich men prosperous and happy. A secular type of virtue is their preoccupation, mostly. In Israel wisdom is more profound, more plebeian, and more religious. But it is never occupied with political virtue or affairs of state. In this respect the wisdom literature stands in contrast to the work of the prophets.

In Job we have this individualism, full-blown. The nation or tribe figures only once in the book (12:23-25). The be-

[5] Pfeiffer, op. cit., dates the book in the time of Jeremiah and believes that it exercised a decisive influence on Second Isaiah, Proverbs, and Psalms.

havior of Job's sons is under scrutiny as a possible explanation of the calamity to them, but Job really stands alone to face his history and his destiny. While there can be no finality about the notion that this individualism of the book had to wait for the development of individualism among the prophets, yet the notion is an interesting and related story. When Eliphaz, Bildad, and Zophar argue that Job's misery is a sure sign that he is paying the penalty for his own sins, they are voicing an orthodox doctrine of retribution which must have been well established in the day of the book. This was not handed down from ancient times intact. It was the end product of the prophetic criticism of life and the unfolding of events in Judah.

Early Hebrews shared the primitive belief that evils are caused by demons and black magic and the sins of the tribe. The prophets had to combat such notions. Jeremiah and Ezekiel found their congregations rationalizing their troubles by saying "In those days they shall no longer say: 'The fathers have eaten sour grapes, and the children's teeth are set on edge.' But every one shall die for his own sin; each man who eats sour grapes, his teeth shall be set on edge" (Jer. 31:29-30). Ezekiel denied it with the proposition, "Behold, all souls are mine; the soul of the father as well as the soul of the son is mine: the soul that sins shall die" (Ezek. 18:4). But it took the national catastrophe to bring the individual Jew to stand alone before Yahweh.

We do not know very much about the political and material aspects of the Jerusalem community during the century and a half which followed the restoration activities of Ezra and Nehemiah. No historian recorded the names and deeds of governors. Perhaps that is because they were not kings, or that little happened of interest to storytellers. The Persian Empire held sway. There was no political independence. The nationalist consciousness, which could be whipped into fanatical fury at a later date, was now dormant. The individual must obey the law and at stated festivals present himself before Yahweh in the Temple to make atonement.

It was an age of great literary activity. Much of the Hebrew Bible belongs to this period and the ancient documents were edited and embellished. The Law was established, re-edited, and supplemented with the Priestly Code. The king's court and nobility were no more, but the Priesthood reigned in the hearts of the people and developed an elaborate and beautiful ceremonial.

The shift in intellectual climate is like that which took place in Greece at a later date when empire quenched the last dim fires of democracy in Athens. The ethical schools of Zeno and Epicurus and the Academy turned their attention away from such problems as produced the *Republic* of Plato and the *Politics* of Aristotle to the definitions of virtue and happiness for the individual Greek.

In times of peace, even a military peace, piety and frugality tend to be rewarded with prosperity, and iniquity of any kind brings retribution fairly sure in its wake. Political opportunity gone, the good man could distinguish himself by his reputation for honesty, charity, and prosperity, and thus the type of piety which we see portrayed in Proverbs, Psalms, and Job became the ideal of the land. And the ideal produced a high type of man, one who is completely honorable in all his dealings (even if "perfect" may be too sharp a word for the Hebrew adjective applied to Job). The doctrine developed is sometimes called "perfectionism." Man can be good if he wants to, and his goodness is sure to be rewarded, and rewards were then primarily thought of in terms of prosperity.

But the ideal was not accepted by all. We hear a great deal about the wicked and ungodly men. They, as in every age, are the men who live by their cleverness. They are powerful and frequently prosperous. The contrast between the pious and the ungodly was very great. Judging from the frequent allusions to them in Psalms and Proverbs, as well as in the Book of Job, the prosperity of wicked men was a worry to the sages no less than the sufferings of the righteous, and the literature provides two separate suggestions in answer to it. A recurrent refrain in the Psalms (37th for instance) is the claim that the prosperity of the wicked is short and sure to be followed by retribution. This has a faint echo in the arguments of Job's friends, but they mostly ignore Job's claim that wicked men are immune from the evils which have overtaken him. They dwell on the dire fate that awaits the ungodly.

A second theme (Psalms 7, 17) comes from noble souls whose integrity and good conscience render them superior to the consideration of the fate of the wicked. In Psalm 73 we have a case where a worshipful experience of God lifts the soul to heights superior to envy and fretful concern over others. As the argument of the Book of Job comes to its climax, we find an achievement of a position similar to these two suggestions, but before that the daring poet has a more direct challenge to the common theory of his time. He raises a doubt about the providence of God. Is it true that the wicked always come to a bad end? Can we be so sure that God is even concerned about the matter, as we are?

As the Persian period came to an end, the march of empires again brought a dire threat to the Jerusalem community. Then appeared a type of literature called apocalyptic because it purports to set forth a sacred revelation about the end of things. The Book of Daniel and Chapters 24-27 of the Book of Isaiah are of this type. Here this problem of retribution and reward is put into the hereafter. At the end, a divine manifestation will bring the righteous to resurrection in which all wrongs will be righted and all virtue rewarded. Job first specifically denies this doctrine (7:8-9; 14:7-12) and then he entertains the notion momentarily (16:19; 19:23-27).

Such is the historical setting in which the Book of Job must be understood.

Picking at the Parts of the Skein

The whole work as it stands in our Bible makes a beautiful edifice. Emil Kraeling looks at it on the analogy of a cathedral. When one steps within, the sections are somewhat loosely joined, but they do not fall apart as some have seemed to imagine. The literary unity of the document has been a major problem for critical students. To mix the metaphor, the doctors have disagreed over the vivisection and the function of the parts, and probably will for generations of commentators to come.

The central "nave" of the structure is a series of poems comprising the symposium between Job and his friends (Chapters 3-31). Here the problem of the piece is set and the argument unfolded. The poetic imagination takes some excursions which are a little hard to fit into the coherent scheme. Some scholars wield a critical knife here and there, finding extraneous stanzas and some verses which may have been added as marginal notes by scribes. Chapters 3-25 unfold a symmetrical discourse which is the series of solid pillars and high-vaulted arches at the center of the whole and supporting all the parts. Even the glosses are valuable decorative vignettes.

Chapters 26-27 appear to have been jumbled somewhat by scribes and editors. It is possible to rearrange them so that a complete third cycle of speeches comes out and a more consistent conclusion to the argument. A simple way to do this is to supplement the brief speech of Bildad in Chapter 25 with the poem about the wonders of God in nature, 26:5-14, although that is not out of place in any of the speeches. Job, then, would have 26:1-4 and 27:1-7 for response. The poems about the fate of the wicked, 27:8-23 and 30:2-8, are inconsistent with Job's sentiments in Chapter 21, so from these we might get a third speech for Zophar, completing the cycle.[6]

Chapter 28 is a poem complete in itself, extolling wisdom but putting the subject in a way hardly compatible with Proverbs 8 and 9. This puts wisdom beyond the reach of man, even superior to God himself. The last verse is thought by many to be a gloss added by some later hand to make the poem consistent with Jewish ideas of revelation. Yet it is possible to find in this beautiful poem the emergence of a basic insight, the point at which "Job's suffering is transmuted into spiritual triumph." [7] Such it is to realize that the ways of suffering are hidden in the inscrutable providence of God and to submit the will to Him by faith, for

> Behold, the fear of the Lord, that is wisdom;
> and to depart from evil is understanding. (28:28)

Here the Book of Job, at any rate, echoes a common refrain of Jewish wisdom: Psalm 111:10; Proverbs 9:10; Ecclesiastes 12:13.

An Ancient Folk Tale

The Hebrew storyteller works in prose; the poet is the philosopher. So we have a long prologue (Chapters 1 and 2) and an epilogue (42:7-17) in prose, containing most of the narrative. The careful reader will observe some striking differences between these and the poetic symposium which raise the question about the unity of the work. One difference has to do with the name of God. Thirty-one times he is called Yahweh in the narrative, only twice in the poems, and these are verses which might be glosses. The poetic words

---

[6] Scholars have exercised great ingenuity in making such reconstructions, with differing and complicated results, and with what seems to this writer as very subjective criteria. The student may find such a shifting of passages in Moffatt's translation. See also Pfeiffer, op. cit., p. 671.

[7] Moses Buttenwieser, The Book of Job (New York: The Macmillan Co., 1925), p. 61.

for God are El, Elohim, Eloah, and Shaddai. This does not strike one so obviously in the English translation, but two other differences do.

Job appears in the narrative as a pious and patient sufferer who clings desperately to his religious faith, and in the end is properly rewarded for it, but when he opens his mouth after the long vigil with his suspicious friends he turns into a vitriolic challenger of every traditional notion about the meaning of life and the ways of God. We wonder about his piety, and his patience evaporates.

Then the two episodes in heaven make a sharp contrast. Satan appears as a direct agent of tragedy, and yet when men are searching heaven and earth for an explanation there is not the slightest hint that such a supernatural being operates at cross-purposes to God and pious souls. In much of the popular folklore of the world, devils have explained all manner of evil, and it could hardly be said that the thought never occurred to Hebrew wise men. Yet the idea offered no solution to our poet.

One intriguing explanation is that the authors were working with an old folk tale about an ancient hero whose story is fully related in the prologue and epilogue. Taken separately, it is a story which satisfies quite well the requirements of the orthodox doctrine that righteousness and faithful piety are always rewarded with prosperity and benign old age. That the story was used for such teaching seems to be indicated by Ezekiel's reference to the righteousness of Job (14:14) and the notice of the patience of Job in the Epistle of James (5:11). This story probably existed in the oral tradition for many generations, becoming not only the vehicle of the orthodox doctrine but also the nucleus around which clustered the questionings of the postexilic community about the problem of evil. With full appreciation of its dramatic quality, the authors separated the story and poured into the tale their poetic struggle with the problem. Or this might have been done by some editor, putting together the works of earlier writers. Perhaps a more common view is that one writer did the prologue and the symposium, but that the epilogue was added by a later hand to bolster the orthodox doctrine, which by no means died out in Judah by the hand of this poet.

Elihu

Hebrew scholars are almost unanimous in assigning the Elihu speeches to an inferior poet. The section probably indicates something of the shock which theologians got from the original poetic symposium—so shocked that one or more tried to compose additional stanzas to refute Job and amend the weakness of the counterargument. Yet the inferiority of these poems may be due to the high level attained by the original poet. We would not cut them out, and as pointed out before, Elihu supplies an important dramatic effect.

Theophany

The speeches of Yahweh also might have come from another hand, but if so, the poet achieves the highest level of quality and power. Anticipations of such a manifestation, however, are to be found in the symposium which make it more probable that the theophany is the final insight of that author (9:32-33; 11:7-10; 16:19; 19:25-27; 23:3-10). Modern interpreters of the book have been sharply divided on the value of these poems to the whole. There is no rational solution of the problem. Some, therefore, see in this section only an impotent collapse to arbitrary power on the part of Job, while others see it as the supreme achievement of religious faith. This question must come up for special consideration later.

For us, the whole stands as a magnificent structure, replete with beauty, pathos, and truth. No doubt a modern literary genius, a Shakespeare or a Goethe, would have created a more unified edifice, but he would have sacrificed insight for symmetry. That is why there is nothing in literature quite equal to the book. We shall take it as it stands in our Bible, and we shall find important contributions in every section.

Purposes

Three questions of a general nature are explored in the Book of Job, and around each of these a great many subordinate problems cluster. The first might be termed a psychological question: just how would a man perform if he were subjected to the test of suffering as was Job? It is sharpened by Satan's cynical doubt, "Does Job fear God for nought?" Are man's piety and morality conditioned by his prosperity, his social position, or his standard of living? These questions are answered in two ways, first in the prologue, and second in the argument. Job at first makes a noble and affirmative answer as he stands the test. It is a sincere and disinterested piety he exhibits. However much we admire his affirmation, we nevertheless feel a deep sympathy with the skepticism which pours from his lips in the second phase when he and his friends excogitate the full issue. This enigma demands a more profound answer than "The LORD gave, the LORD has taken away; blessed be the name of the LORD."

So the question turns from man to God and is posed for the theologian: what sort of world is this, and what kind of deity rules over it, in which just and innocent people suffer the torments of hell? Or is there such a thing as an innocent man? If not, what is the relation of guilt to suffering? This is the major problem of the book and likewise the central problem of all religious philosophy.

Then the Job story confronts us throughout with the question: what is religion? How does it enable man to face and interpret the evil of existence? Does it offer a workable solution of the problem of evil? Nowhere is this over-all question raised in precisely those terms, but it certainly sustains the quest of the poets and all those redactors and editors who put the document together. At the formative stage of our religious faith, Job made a basic contribution which still commands consideration and respect.

The purpose in the subsequent chapters of this book will be to explore the problem as it unfolds in the second question and to discover some of the philosophical answers to it. Then we shall find in Job a series of practical suggestions for facing the evil of life, a sort of pragmatic answer to the problem, which is the genius of our religion.

THE BOOK OF JOB IN OLD TESTAMENT CHRONOLOGY

1220 B.C., Probable date of the Exodus under Moses.

1200–1028, Period of invasion and conquest of Palestine.

1013–933, Reigns of David and Solomon, founding of the kingdom.

722, Fall of Samaria to Assyria, disappearance of northern tribes.

8th Century, Rise of the literary prophets: Amos, Hosea, Isaiah, Micah.

626–585, The prophet Jeremiah.

586, Destruction of Jerusalem and exile in Babylon.

539, Persian conquest of Babylon under Cyrus.

538, Cyrus granted permission for return of exiles to Jerusalem.

592–570, Ezekiel, prophet of the Exile.

About 536, Oracles of Second Isaiah (Chapters 40-55), prophet of the Return.

538–331, The Persian period in which many Old Testament documents were written, including the Book of Job, about 400.

331, Conquest of Persia by Alexander, beginning of the Greek period.

168, Attempt of Antiochus Epiphanes to suppress the Jewish religion, beginning of the Maccabaean period.

167, The Book of Daniel and flowering of apocalyptic literature.

(Based on "The Chronology of the Old Testament" by Elmer A. Leslie in *The Abingdon Bible Commentary* (New York: The Abingdon Press, 1929).)

Chapter 3

JOB'S GOD AND HIS UNIVERSE

The Semites lived in a beautiful and fearsome world. Semitic sages were cosmologists, speculators about the kind of universe man lives in, long before they became devotees of the monotheistic religious faith; and the unity and beauty of the cosmos which they conceived undoubtedly had much to contribute to the rise of belief in a single creative and ruling deity. In fact, monotheism as it has come down to us in Western religious thought, is inextricably entwined with cosmology. The Christian faith was unfolded within this Semitic world view and it has been transferred to two others, the Ptolemaic and the Copernican, which in turn replaced it; and in our own time that faith is running into certain doubts just because of the difficulty of cosmology today.

Early Babylonian Mythology.

In the vast library of cuneiform literature uncovered at the ancient site of Nineveh about a century ago, two cosmological poems came to light which carry our knowledge of such speculations back for a thousand or more years in Babylonia and Assyria before Hebrew literature began. These are the Gilgamesh Epic, which contains a story of the flood, and the series of clay tablets which set forth the account of creation. The world was created out of primeval chaos by a struggle between the gods of light and the demons of chaos which were led by the monster Tiamat. Bel-Marduk, the sun god, led the battle for the gods of light, and defeated Tiamat, both by his prowess and his superior cleverness. When Tia-mat opened her mouth to utter a magical incantation, her one invincible weapon, Bel-Marduk turned loose the east wind which entered her mouth and inflated her belly to great size. Then with his spear he thrust her through and went to work on the carcass. The lower part he separated for the earth, and out of the upper section he fashioned the dome of heaven. Then he put Apsu, the great deep, in his proper place and set up bars to hold back the waters. From this source, water, ocean, and the monsters of the deep stand for chaos in all Semitic poetry. Man was created by Bel-Marduk to provide a plaything for the gods so they would not get too restless under the dictatorial rule of the sun god. He drew the blood of Kingu, consort of Tiamat and mingled it with the dust of the ground.

This mythology, in many variations and in numerous dia-lects, must have circulated for countless generations among the tribes which surrounded the Arabian Desert and migrated along the Fertile Crescent. Shorn of its primitive magic and most of its demonic crudity, we have the cosmic speculations emerging in the Bible as the picture of the world in which God operates. One might read much of the Old Testament, to be sure, the historical books, the law books, and the proph-ets, without finding it except as it is presupposed. The early prophets and all the literature inspired by them were con-cerned with man's political activities, until the time of the exile, and then we find the writer of the Second Isaiah relating Yahweh to all nations and the cosmos in which they dwell. He lived in Babylon. But the reader of Genesis 1-11, Psalms 8; 19:1-6; 29; 104; 147; 148, Proverbs 8:22-31, and the Book of Job finds this world view emerging in clear outlines. The Hebrew concept of God is involved with it. We do not find cosmology here in the scientific sense. There is no effort to set forth the workings of nature for their own sake. Every-thing is the manifestation of God in some form.

The heavens are telling the glory of God;
and the firmament proclaims his handiwork.
Day to day pours forth speech,
and night to night declares knowledge. (Ps. 19:1-2)

In Job, God and the cosmos are inextricably involved in the problem of the book. Lightning and a tornado and a foul disease have combined with the evil depredations of men to reduce the saint to his desperation. And the author is a profound scholar. He has explored nature from the height of heaven to the depth of Sheol, and all the lore of Egypt and Persia as well as that of Babylonia. In one of Job's speeches (12:13-25), God appears as the ruler of nations, as in the prophets, but primarily the problem of this thinker is the individual man, set in the midst of nature and his relation to the God who rules there.

The Job Cosmos

The world in which the ancient Hebrews lived is a marvelous fabrication out of the raw sense experience which sight, sound, and touch bring to man. The earth is a solid irregular mass whose cornerstone and foundations are suspended upon empty space (26:7; 38:4-7). No Titan Atlas is needed to hold it up, for the Almighty power sustains it from above. Water surrounds it below and a watery mist above, symbols of chaos, but land boundaries have been set to keep back the floods of the great deep which still pound away as a constant threat to overwhelm the puny denizens of the land (26:10-12; 3:8; 7:12; 38:8-11; 41:31). Mountains are a refuge from the waters which frequently overtake the valleys, but even these can be upset by God in his wrath when he shakes the earth (9:5-6; 26:11). Soil erosion is a problem to Job, as it is to the economic philosophers of America's Department of Agriculture (14:18-19). A feeling of fearful awe is aroused in our poet when he thinks of the demonic powers of chaos.

Tiamat still lives in the Rahab of the Bible; the monster
Leviathan still swims in the great deep and may be roused
up by incantation (3:8; 41), but a watch has been set over
him (7:12). God has subdued all these, and they, rather than
man, are his playthings (Ps. 104:26).[1] His cleverness, like
that of Bel-Marduk, has smitten through Rahab (26:12) and
her helpers stoop and slink under his anger (9:13).

The distant mountains are pillars on which God has
stretched out the heavens as a great dome like a molten mir-
ror (26:11; 37:18). He has fixed the course of the sun and
moon and garnished the heavens with stars. He leads forth
the great constellations, the Pleiades, Orion, the Mazzaroth,
and the Bear in their proper seasons (9:2-13; 26:13; 38:31-33).
God commands the dayspring to come forth and grip the ends
of the earth (38:12-13). He fixes the dwelling place of light
and darkness (38:19-21); and the poet dwells on the distinction between these with something like the far-off echo of
Zarathustra (3:4-10), although darkness is not a devil like
Ahriman, but pure nonbeing or apathy. In the heavens God
has fixed the storehouses of snow and hail which he reserves
for weapons of intervention in battle (38:22-23). The wind
is his breath, and it may sooth the spirit of man in cooling
zephyrs or become an icy blast (4:9). He stores water in the
cloud to turn loose when he will (5:10; 12:15), and utters his
voice in the thunder. He hurls lightning almost as arbitrarily
as the Olympian Zeus (37:1-13).

At the height of the heavenly dome, God has his throne
and he walks about on the vault. Job wonders if the thick
clouds do not cover him so that he does not always see what
is going on down below (26:9; 22:12-14), but the wonder does
not turn to doubt. Though the vault is very high and Sheol
is very deep, the all-seeing eye penetrates through so that

[1] See Elmer A. Leslie's interpretation of this Psalm in his *The Psalms*
(New York: Abingdon-Cokesbury Press, 1949). Pages 131-152 deal with the
nature Psalms.

nothing happens without his knowing (11:7-12). Nothing in the natural world operates independently of him. All living creatures will instruct one about God (12:7-10). The beasts are a marvelous display of his handiwork (38:39-39:30), and even the stones of the field can furnish a link with the plan of the Almighty (5:23).

Is God the creator of all this majesty? There is no account of creation itself in the book, but the Genesis story is probably assumed. Once, in the words of Job, it is clearly stated that Yahweh wrought all this (12:9), and Elihu declares that God is man's maker (35:10). In accordance with wisdom, God designed and measured the edifice and established the ordinances by which the parts operate (28:23-27; 38:33; cf. Proverbs 8:22-31). There is no doctrine of creation out of nothing. In fact, that notion which became current among the Early Church Fathers does not appear in the Old Testament. The earliest statement of it seems to be in the Greek version of II Maccabees, Chapter 7. According to Job, there was both chaos and the principles of wisdom to start with; they are eternal. Wisdom, like the Greek *Logos*, was in the beginning with God and all things were made according to it (28:23-27), but wisdom is never personified like St. John's *Word* (John 1:2).

God and Man

The place of man in this cosmos is the thing which sharpens the problem of Job and God's dealings with him. Man's lot is bad. He lives in a house of clay and his foundation is in the dust (4:19). He is born to trouble as surely as sparks fly upward (5:7). God is the only holy one and nothing in heaven or earth is pure by comparison (4:17-20). All the evils which afflict man come as a direct visitation of the Almighty. "If it is not he, who then is it?" (9:17-24; 5:17; 16:11). Job ponders his situation in words of deep penetration:

> What is man, that thou dost make so much of him,
>   and that thou dost set thy mind upon him,
> dost visit him every morning,
>   and test him every moment? (7:17-18)

The problem does not present itself in quite such a fashion to modern man because of the nearness of God to Job and the remoteness of God from us. As James McKechnie cleverly states the matter, "Such concepts as chance, laws of nature, secondary causes—concepts by which we screen ourselves in thought from the naked flash of omnipotence—were foreign to Job's scheme of thought." [2]

The doctrines of original sin and total depravity had not then been formulated, but Eliphaz, the Puritan of the drama, lays the foundations for them in his solemn warning that we must not blaspheme against the holy name by challenging divine goodness. We should remember that we are mere creatures, and thus sin and the need for repentance are inevitable:

> What is man, that he can be clean?
>   Or he that is born of a woman, that he can be righteous?
> Behold, God puts no trust in his holy ones,
>   and the heavens are not clean in his sight;
> how much less one who is abominable and corrupt,
>   a man who drinks iniquity like water! (15:14-16)

Moreover, the life of man is short and full of misery and wretchedness. He is crushed like the moth, and perishes forever without anyone's giving serious heed to it (4:19-20). He passes from earth to the dismal shades of Sheol, the cavernous abode of darkness under the earth, and comes up no more (7:9). God is the keeper of the gates (38:17), and even there one finds no place to hide from his scrutiny, for its darkness is naked before him (14:13; 26:6). The poet is much occupied with the problem of death and it must concern us in a later chapter.

[2] James McKechnie, *Job* (New York: George H. Doran Co., 1927), p. 69.

With all God's control of the forces that play around man and bring him to destruction, yet Job longs for a more personal contact which eludes him:

> Oh, that I knew where I might find him,
>   that I might come even to his seat!
> I would lay my case before him
>   and fill my mouth with arguments.
> I would learn what he would answer me,
>   and understand what he would say to me.
>
> .   .   .   .
>
> Behold, I go forward, but he is not there;
>   and backward, but I cannot perceive him;
> on the left hand I seek him, but I cannot behold him;
>   I turn to the right hand, but I cannot see him. (23:3-5, 8-9)

Our poet was perhaps too much occupied with the outer search into the nature of things. Is it not ever thus when man has sought for God in nature alone? Zophar pointed that out to Job (11:7). He seems never to have looked where the prophets found God, in history and in the still small voice within (I Kings 19:12). God spoke to Job in the roaring thunder and the moaning of the whirlwind. The modern man of faith is better represented by Tennyson:

> I found Him not in world or sun,
>   Or eagle's wing, or insect's eye;
>   Nor thro' the questions men may try,
> The petty cobwebs we have spun:
>
> If e'er when faith had fall'n asleep,
>   I heard a voice 'believe no more'
>   And heard an ever-breaking shore
> That tumbled in the Godless deep;
>
> A warmth within the breast would melt
>   The freezing reason's colder part,
>   And like a man in wrath the heart
> Stood up and answer'd 'I have felt.'
>
> (*In Memoriam*, cxxiv)

Yet there is a lighter and brighter side for the Job poet also. Life itself is the breath of the Almighty (33:4). There is a kind of deliverance which comes only to benighted souls through suffering (5:17-22; 36:10-15). Visions are a divine communication to man's spirit (4:12-16; 33:14-16), although these can be terrifying as well as awe-inspiring (7:13-14). God gives song in the night (35:10), and if man listens carefully perchance he may hear the morning stars sing together and all the sons of God shout for joy (38:7). So the moods of life alternate as wandering clouds alter the face of the sky (36:29).

Where does all this bring us in the conception of God? Job certainly does not stand at the pinnacle of the Old Testament theology, but the book accomplishes one thing which is in advance of the other literature of Israel and is definitive for all of Western tradition since. His God is the Creator and Ruler of the cosmos. He is all-powerful, all-wise, and everywhere present in the activities of this universe.

In one decisive particular, Job falls short of the prophetic conception. The poets had not fully absorbed the great insights of that tradition. We have already indicated one point: the preoccupation with the outward effects of deity, and the failure to sense the inwardness of the God consciousness. The God of the prophets was apprehended in history and the moral purposes of man. The God of the cosmos shows himself in the awe-inspiring displays of nature. The God of history has his wrathful aspects, too, but he is primarily experienced in the inward parts, the covenant written upon the heart, and in terms of love.

The Job authors overlooked Hosea, one of the oldest of the prophets. He had a struggle with suffering and evil, in some ways more poignant, if not more dramatic, than the sufferings of Job. In the Samaria of the eighth century, the ancient institution of prostitution flourished and was hallowed by the sanctuaries. Hosea may have taken Gomer from the retinue of sacred prostitutes to be his wife, and at the command of Yahweh, in the spirit of all true lovers.[3] Gomer lived with him long enough to bear him three children, and then she heard the call of the wild and went back to the life of harlotry. After the bloom and vigor of youth were gone, she fell on the inevitable evil days, coming at last to slavery. She was on the auction block, and again at the command of Yahweh, Hosea paid the redemption price and reinstated her in his home.

The prophet saw in this tragic experience the analogy for the unhappy lot of his countrymen, and he looked into his own heart for an intuition about the nature of Yahweh. Israel is like the wife of whoredom. She has spurned all the patient wooing of Yahweh and "gone a-whoring after other gods." And she has fallen into all the social and moral evils natural to it. Cruelty and treachery and exploitation are rife in the land. She burns incense in holy places, but it only covers the stench of a brothel. The sweet fragrance of a home is lacking. Yet if Israel will return and substitute righteous living for the mockery of heathen rites, Yahweh will love her as a new bride.

Perhaps, however, we should overlook the failure of the Job poets to apprehend the meaning of this doctrine that God is love, for it has taken many centuries of human experience, and finally the loving sacrifice of the Son of God himself, to break that revelation upon the world. And then, too, the prophets did not settle the problem of Job, even with their concept of divine love, and in a sense their doctrine of divine justice precipitated the problem, as indicated before. If God is loving as well as just, why do innocent people suffer, as Hosea, Jeremiah, and Job did?

[3] In his *Meet Amos and Hosea* (New York: Harper & Bros., 1945), pp. 81 ff., Rolland Emerson Wolfe has cast doubt on the authenticity of this story on the ground that the text bears the marks of later interpreters of Hosea's oracles in the light of subsequent Jewish history. This is plausible enough, although we prefer to follow the traditional interpretation of the document as it stands. The critical account does not change the main impact of Hosea's doctrine of love.

God and No-God

We may here remark upon the curious point that the Job writers never raise a doubt as to the being of God. In bitter anguish Job cries out against the ways of God, charging him with unjust tormenting, yet he never questions his existence or his omnipotence. In this he shares the spirit of the Hebrew faith. Nowhere in the Scriptures is there a formal argument for the existence of God or any statement of a pure atheism. To the Hebrews, only 'the fool says in his heart, 'There is no God.' They are corrupt, they do abominable deeds, there is none that does good" (Psalm 14:1). "The fool says in his heart, 'There is no God.' They are corrupt, doing abominable iniquity; there is none that does good" (Psalm 53:1).

We are too much under the influence of Greek ways of thinking to be so harsh with the honest doubter today. The Greeks have taught us that it is possible to have a rational set of values which are quite independent of theology; and one of our heroes, Socrates, was put to death in Athens by drinking the hemlock, a story of martyrdom second only to the story of Calvary, because he dared to cast doubt upon the existence of the popular gods.

The first classical document to give Western thought an atheistic answer to the problem of evil was directly influenced by Greek naturalism. It is the long Latin poem, *De Rerum Natura* (Concerning the Nature of Things), by Lucretius. This is a didactic work, in many ways comparable to Job, although without dialogue or dramatic setting. Lucretius is a devotee of the Epicurean pleasure philosophy, but he finds no lasting pleasure, no supreme bliss. The work is a deeply pessimistic review of the evils of man's existence, reflecting the basic hopelessness of Greek thought, for there is no ultimate meaning or solution. In fact, the work might be described as a denial of all ultimates except matter and motion.

Lucretius opens with a paean to Venus, the very earthy goddess of love. Her virtues, which are the delights of love in the sense of *eros* and devotion to beauty of form, turn out to be a sort of madness rather than rational pleasure or happiness. He closes the poem with a description of the horrors of a plague which rivals the Book of Lamentations in realism. The pessimism is not even relieved by a gentle cynicism like that to be found in the Book of Ecclesiastes. One must have a strain of ultimate optimism, like the Jews, to be a true cynic.

The popular pagan world was much occupied with the fears of death and a cluster of superstitions which surrounded it. In a passage which reminds us of the skepticism of Job, Lucretius argues that if lightning is caused by Jupiter, hurling the fire of heaven wherever he is minded, why doesn't he single out some notorious sinner as a lesson to man? Why is he as likely to pick out some innocent victim,

> he whose conscience is burdened with no foul offense, innocent though he be, wrapped and enveloped in the flames, in a moment caught up by the whirlwind and fire of heaven? [4]

Man's dream experience and the mysterious causes of things give people the substance of religious thought. Much in the spirit of the prophets, he condemns the fear-breeding propitiations by which the popular cults bind the soul of men to superstitions. It is a better form of piety "rather to be able to look at all things with a mind at peace."

The peaceful mind, for Lucretius, is to be achieved by the scientific analysis of nature and the contemplation of natural philosophy. All things are thus seen to be caused by the motion of atomic particles in empty space. The world

[4] Quotations from the Munro translation, pp. 200 and 191, respectively, in W. J. Oates (ed.) *The Stoic and Epicurean Philosophers* (New York: Random House, Inc., 1940).

has not been made by divine power, "so great are the defects with which it stands encumbered." The spirit world, like the soul of man, is only the chance production of nature. Such are the popular gods, whose existence he does not deny. But there is no supernatural order determining the origin or destiny of man. Birth is a fortuitous arrangement of atoms, and death is their simple dissolution.

> Mankind therefore ever toils vainly and to no purpose
> and wastes life in groundless cares,
> because sure enough they have not learnt what is the true end
> of getting,
> and up to what point genuine pleasure goes on increasing.

Lucretius' poem should be characterized simply as one reaction to the problem. It is no solution. One who makes a study of it should also review the Latin philosophy of Boethius in his *The Consolation of Philosophy*, a work which had great influence upon Christianity during the Middle Ages. Boethius was a poet and philosopher whose cruel imprisonment, torture, and execution, in the sixth century, by Theodoric, king of the Ostrogoths, is an episode in the final tragedy of the noble Roman. He sought to preserve the best of pagan culture at the time of barbarian ascendency, and the charge of treason was inevitable because of the faithful obedience he gave to his conscience. Lucretius failed to see that man lives in two worlds, the world of nature and the realm of freedom. If he were merely a machine, or even an animal (though that raises some unsolved questions), there would be no problem. Man's suffering is acute, and his tragedy is complete, precisely because he is a free spirit possessed of dreams and purposes and ideals and conscience and a sense of guilt, as well as the power of reason. Boethius is the more profound because he had discovered this truth from the Hebrew-Christian tradition, and in turn he gave to the Christian world a book which helped it to absorb the nobler elements in Greek philosophy.

Truly amazing is the popularity of this atheistic reaction to the evil of existence in modern times, even in recent interpretations of the Book of Job. In the *Undying Fire*,[5] H. G. Wells has given us a modern story on the Job pattern. His Job is a Mr. Huss, headmaster of a school, who has lost his only son in the war and is smitten with cancer. As he prepares to go under the knife, three directors of the school arrive, just ahead of the surgeon, to break the news that he is to be relieved of his duties because of his progressive educational philosophy. He sees the ideals of a lifetime fading. The sickroom is turned into an ash heap, and the dialogue revives the problem of Job. Eliphaz, Bildad, and Zophar are there, defenders of traditional orthodox theories of education and social life, and the surgeon arrives to take the role of Elihu. Mr. Wells is too much a child of our times to be able to produce a theophany, and in complete harmony with the spirit of the day, he makes Mr. Huss say: "Where we had thought a god, somehow akin to ourselves, ruled in the universe, it may be there is nothing but black emptiness and a coldness worse than cruelty."

The best of such efforts is *A Modern Job*,[6] written by a French philosopher who lived in Holland, M. Étienne Giran. Descendants of the ancient patriarchs of the drama in the land of Uz, and bearing the same names, gather on the banks of a canal to commune with Job, a modern business man whose soul has been reduced to despair by a set of modern-type calamities. Job takes the role of the modern atheist and discomfits Eliphaz, whose theology is the traditional notion of the omnipotent deity, dispenser of exact retribution, which he defends even in the sufferings of Christ for the sins of the world. Then Bildad comes in with a modern type of dualism in which the omnipotence of God is denied because of powers over which he has no control. This is found inade-

[5] (New York: The Macmillan Co., 1919).
[6] (Chicago: Open Court Publishing Co., 1916).

quate, but Job finally subsides into silence as Zophar unfolds
a mystic and humanistic pantheism in the modern spirit.
Elihu, in the person of the old servant, has not quite understood the philosophical subtleties, but he distils the essence
of wisdom by recalling the words of the Gospel of St. John,
"This is my commandment, that you love one another."
The story ends with Job absorbing the beauty of the evening
sun, painting the canal into a river of gold, as a substitute for
the theophany, and with a question, rather than a theophany,
and a repentance, "Was God, . . . restoring to him the very
treasures of life that blind circumstance had snatched from
his grasp?"

None of this atheism appears in Job. The ancient skeptic
challenges the goodness of God. Modernism doubts the
existence of God. Perhaps the two are not so far apart. Both
are concerned with the ultimate status of values, and both
answer in a similar spirit by making the ruling forces in the
universe either indifferent or hostile to them. On most of
the atheist philosophers of today we might pass the same
judgment which W. E. Garrison passed on the writer of a
contemporary volume: "His verdict in favor of materialism
is determined less by what he has learned by the scientific
study of fossils than by what he imagines about what God
would be and do—if there were a God." [7]

After we have exhausted our philosophies, we may con-
cede that the Hebrews were right. Reasoning will never
extirpate the idea of God from the human heart; neither will
theory put his existence beyond the reach of doubt. He is
above and beyond and before all proof. His Word is the
logic of proof itself; but he is not to be proved; he is to be
accepted. He is not demonstrated; he is discovered. From
the standpoint of philosophy, the idea of God will always be
a dogma. All the proof man needs is in his own heart, in his

[7] From a book review in The Christian Century (January 11, 1950), p.
50.

consciousness of freedom and insufficiency, in his dependence upon spiritual powers beyond himself. All the rational arguments for God are important in modern philosophy, for in the modern temper, faith cannot be divorced from reason; but in the last analysis they rest upon the subjective feeling and will which Kant called the practical reason. And this is the Biblical proof of God which underlies the thought of Job. He realizes that he is only a creature, yet more than a mere animal. Beyond are the forces that mold his destiny, and to deny their personal reality, as is the fashion of modern sophistication, never enters the poets' thought.

Is God One and Personal?

God, for Job, not only is but he is one. Our poet-philosopher is a strict monotheist; there is no place in his system for rival deities. He understands the spell cast by the sun in its early morning splendor upon the spirits of his ancient ancestors in the East, and the majestic moon as it moves across the face of the night. But he suppresses the glow of admiration. For his mouth to kiss his hand in their direction would be a denial of the God that is above and to whom they are subject (31:26-28).[8] Here is the only reference to any of the ancient forms of idolatry.

The rigidness and sublimity of his monotheism is accentuated by the fact that Job never thinks to credit his suffering to the work of some power rival to God. Satanic dualism, which is such an easy and attractive solution of the problem, seems never to have taken hold of the poet's imagination. Satan remains in the supernal background, a permissive agent, and God alone is responsible, not only for the evils in nature but even for the sinner and his evil work. The poet is very positive about this: the deceived and the deceiver are both alike his (12:16).

[8] In this section I am indebted to A. S. Peake's *Job* in The New Century Bible (Edinburgh: T. C. & E. C. Jack, 1904), pp. 5 and 270.

Some critics have raised a question about Job's God being a personal God. Even though he is constantly referred to in concrete personal terms, such as the eyes, hands, arms, and heart of God, these are poetic metaphors, and important personal qualities are wanting in the concept. Suffering often gives man a feeling of remoteness from God, and that is especially true when it is interpreted as an act of punishment. Punishment in itself is a purposive and personal relation, but Job finds it difficult to get on terms of understanding with him:

> For he is not a man as I am, that I might answer him,
>   that we should come to trial together.
> There is no umpire between us,
>   who might lay his hand upon us both. (9:32-33)

The God of Job is primarily a cosmic force, and apart from the historical context of the Bible he would probably be as impersonal as Aristotle's prime mover. He acquires unity from the marvelous scheme of things. The causes of things are divine purposes but they are inscrutable. Like every purely cosmic God, this falls short of a truly personalistic concept. Yet Job's cosmic deity, united in the Old Testament with the prophetic God of history and human affairs, acquired the thoroughgoing personalization which was completed in the New Testament concept of fatherhood. The personal theism of the Christian faith would hardly have been possible without this combination.[9]

Cosmology Then and Now

A strange and enchanting, though somewhat somber, picture of the universe we have in the Bible! Ptolemaic, Copernican, and Newtonian cosmologies have come and gone since that neat and simple conception of the childhood of

[9] Robert H. Pfeiffer, in his Introduction to the Old Testament (New York: Harper & Bros., 1941), p. 703, discusses this matter but hardly gives enough credit to the influence of Job.

scientific investigation and human reflection. Today we can hardly be said to have a cosmology in that ancient sense, although we use some vague terms to characterize our general understanding of the world and the heavens. We speak of *relativity* and in time we may come to name Einstein in connection with all this, as we do those other mathematicians who constructed the cosmologies of the past.

We speak of the stars in galaxies, one upon another, and some believe that their motion is an expansion through endless space. Any schoolboy can look at a photograph of a nebula which was produced by the light rays disturbing the molecular structure of the film after traveling a distance of hundreds of millions of light-years. Exactly how to interpret the known facts, nobody seems to know, although human speculation never ceases, but the mood which our world induces in many modern reflective souls is like the disillusionment of Thomas Hood's maturity:

> I remember, I remember
> The fir-trees dark and high;
> I used to think their slender tops
> Were close against the sky:
> It was a childish ignorance,
> But now 'tis little joy
> To know I'm farther off from heaven
> Than when I was a boy.

Biblical cosmology was constructed out of the imagery of man's common experience, what he could see, hear, and touch; and God was intimately concerned with every part as designer and maker. After Biblical times, in the Western world the mathematicians took over, and as the cosmos has been progressively reduced to mathematical formulae and scientific law, God's place in it has become more and more problematical. First, Greek science replaced the Semitic world view with the Ptolemaic system. This removed God to the outer sphere of the fixed stars which enclose the heavens, and the perfect motion which he communicated to that circle was thought of as the cause of all motions within, down to the earth at the center. Copernicus saw that the earth was in motion, and he worked out a new set of simplified formulae with the sun at the center. Then Kepler's laws of motion, Galileo's mechanics, and Descartes' vortices were combined and reduced to the formula of gravity by Newton, and the universe became completely self-running. In all this time, the development of Christian theology was closely correlated with these cosmologies. God's omniscience and omnipotence were expressed in the cosmos, and the neat certainty of it made the theology more secure. God's benevolence and love were related to history and the plan for man's redemption. The close tie with cosmology can be seen in all the great theological systems, those of St. Augustine, St. Thomas Aquinas, and Calvin; nowhere more specifically than in Calvin's *Institutes of the Christian Religion.*

The Newtonian world view did not break this tie, but for three hundred years it gave to mechanism a deep rooting in modern thought. Mechanism simply means the explanation of the ways of things without reference to the design or purposes of any mind or spiritual powers. This is not the place to review all the difficulties of theology in the modern scientific world. We point only to the way theology is related to the problem of cosmology.

In our century we look back upon the simplicities of these older cosmologies with some nostalgia: the glorious thirteenth century with the cosmos of Dante, the scholastic doctrines of man and God, and Gothic art; the Age of Reason, with its great idealisms and its dream of the freedom of man. For a revolution has overtaken us greater than that which upset Dante's world when the teachings of Copernicus were brought to Florence. Evolution has revolutionized man's understanding of life and time. Its interpretation of life as a struggle for survival has greatly disturbed traditional solutions of the problem of evil. Relativity is a new theory about space time and motion, but it is not a new cosmology; rather, it is an instrument for the mathematical interpretation of scientific processes, and so far has been more useful in the penetration and explosion of the atom than in speculations about the nature of the universe.

Cosmology has not only become more difficult but perhaps impossible under the expanded scientific outlook. It has been replaced by metaphysics. This is the attempt to give meaning to the nature of things as they exist for us in experience. There has always been metaphysics, too, but it has never been so closely allied to theology as cosmology. While it cannot be said that these new scientific theories have directly aided the old theology, yet it can be claimed that they have unseated the old mechanism and materialism.

The late Herbert Wildon Carr was one of the first philosophers of this century to grasp the significance of the relativity theories for metaphysics. When facing death in 1931, he wrote these words:

> My life has been lived through the great revolution and the time has come for my *nunc dimittis*, and if I cannot rejoice that "mine eyes have seen thy salvation," at least I have lived to see the leading exponents of pure science reproached as idealist philosophers.[10]

Is God Finite?

To relate this matter finally to modern theism one must mention the current fashion of facing the problem of evil by surrender of the attribute of absoluteness in the Deity. It may fairly be said that most recent philosophical theologians who take seriously the implications of modern science, and try to make the God concept conform to them, have qualified in some way the notion of omnipotence, as that is implied in the

[10] Memoir to Professor Carr by Ralph Tyler Flewelling in *The Personalist* (January, 1932), p. 7.

word "Almighty" of Job and later developed in medieval theology.

No difficulty of this sort confronts the faith of those who remain content with the similes and analogies of Biblical thought. There are very many who are still insulated from the problems and methods of modern science as they affect theology. Then there are many who have been exposed and found science to be a false Messiah. So all the traditional orthodoxies flourish today, some of them modified as neo-orthodoxy.

There is nothing entirely new in theology and metaphysics and the differences between the absolutists and the finitists today go back to the distinction between Aristotle and Plato. The Christian tradition of absolutism followed the Biblical doctrine of creation and Aristotle's doctrine of God as the prime mover, and thus God was made the ultimate causal ground of everything, in the orthodox doctrine of omnipotence. Plato's God, on the other hand, was the Idea of the Good, and in the Republic he made it a heresy for anyone to say that God is the cause of the evil.

Alfred North Whitehead has influenced a whole school of theological leaders by deserting the traditional dogmas of creation and omnipotence, and by the development of an original and positive type of Platonic theology. God is the causal ground for the continuous processes which bring concrete good to pass. As one of his best interpreters puts the matter, God "enters into each creative phase not as the Creator but rather as the principle of limitation. He is not responsible for the evil. He does not create the world but saves it." [11]

There is also a practical religious question involved in the argument. What is it that people worship? Do they bow

[11] Julius Seelye Bixler, "Whitehead's Philosophy of Religion" in The Philosophy of Alfred North Whitehead: The Library of Living Philosophers, Vol. III, Edited by Paul Arthur Schilpp (Evanston: Northwestern University, 1941), p. 494. The same volume includes an essay by Charles Hartshorne on "Whitehead's Idea of God."

before naked power? Or, do they adore the highest good? Edgar S. Brightman, the most eloquent expounder of this modern finitism, takes the position that "God is worshipped not because he is omnipotent, but because he is good." [12] But the situation seems to be equivocal and perhaps paradoxical, for there are two impulses involved in man's religious motives. People adore the ideal, but they also fear and propitiate the powers. A God that is good but shorn of power is hardly an object of worship. The Greeks pitied and praised Prometheus but built their altars to Zeus. Even the good God of the finite theology must be sufficiently powerful to be the master of man's destiny, and it would seem that so long as religion is to be monotheistic it must cling to a concept of omnipotence.

Brightman and the personalists define God as the supreme Person, the creative power in all goodness, and sufficiently powerful to merit all man's devotion. But those who follow this idea of finiteness account for the evils of existence on the ground of a psychological Given in God which stands as obstruction to the perfect realization of his will. This is not unlike the nonbeing of Plato, which he held to be the obstruction to the creative Idea of the Good.

Again we must say that there is none of this in the Book of Job. The poets never contemplated either the nonexistence of God nor any concepts of limitation. He is the Almighty. His justice is in question, but not his power.

[12] A *Philosophy of Religion* (New York: Prentice-Hall, Inc., 1940), p. 302. Chapters viii-x are a thorough exposition of the whole problem. On pp. 295-301 he gives an impressive list of modern thinkers who have advocated the doctrine of a finite God. Another recent defense of the limited God idea is by Arthur W. Munk, *History and God* (New York: The Ronald Press Co., 1952), Chapter 8.

Chapter 4

JOB'S SATAN AND OTHER ANCIENT DEMONS

Satan, as he appears in the prologue of the Book of Job, is the most intriguing devil in the world's literature; not the most profound or the most vicious, but by all odds the most exciting. What that Satan became in the myth-making tradition of the Western world will be the substance of our exposition in this chapter and the next.

The scene is only a flash, a short short. The curtain is pulled back upon the throne of heaven. As the calendar rolls round, the day comes when the divine beings assemble for council before Yahweh. We are given a glimpse of these sessions. The "sons of God" are beings who belong to the order of divinity, literally, the "sons of the Elohim," which might be translated, the "sons of deity."

The Satan Idea in the Old Testament

A scene in the earlier Book of the Kings gives us a similar glimpse of the throne of heaven (I Kings 22:19-23). The prophet Micaiah has a vision of Yahweh, with all the host of heaven assembled, calling for some ingenious device for enticing Ahab to his doom at Ramoth-gilead. Ahab, the king of Israel, is frantically calling on the prophets for advice on the campaign, and the gods are against him. After several suggestions, one spirit comes forward with the offer to go and be a lying spirit in the mouth of the other prophets, and it is done. His function is that of "The Satan," but he is not so named.

These same heavenly beings are mentioned in another Old Testament passage (Genesis 6:1-4), which has a curious turn. The tale is a very ancient one, reflecting primitive folklore about the cohabitation of gods and human beings, such as may also be seen in the eleventh book of Homer's *Odyssey*. These "sons of God" observe that the daughters of men are very fair and take them for wives, and the children born to them are the Nephilim or giants and ancient men of renown in the earth. It is not on the face of the story that this *affaire d'amour* was understood as evil at first, but it was placed just before the Flood story in the editing of the ancient documents and came to be construed as an explanation of that wickedness which was very great in the earth before the Deluge. In the apocryphal Book of Enoch, this tale is taken as an explanation of the origin of moral evil, a theory which was a great favorite of late rabbinical interpreters also, and it matched the asceticism of some Early Church Fathers who considered lust the origin of sin and regarded the Nephilim as demons.

According to Jewish apocalyptic writers who belong to a later period than the Book of Job, it appears that these heavenly beings participate in the divine government of the earth. They are assigned to geographic areas and each is held accountable to Yahweh for the way human affairs progress (Daniel 10:13, 20; 12:1; Isaiah 24:21-22). Such a provincial system would account for periodic council meetings when these administrative angels are called to report.

Among these heavenly beings comes one who is assigned to no province. His task is a general function, not an administrative one. He is a restless spirit who travels to and fro and up and down on the earth. He is called The Satan, which means The Adversary, or more specifically, The Accuser. Satan has not yet become a proper name, nor is this creature yet the full-fledged Devil.

Popular thought at the time seems to have entertained the notion that Yahweh maintains a class of Satans or Adversaries ever at hand to attend to the business of prosecuting evil in accordance with divine justice. All who appear in the Old Testament have a specific purpose as such. In fact, the word "satan" is a common noun in Hebrew and is frequently used to indicate an adversary, such as an enemy in battle (Numbers 10:9). Three times it is used this way in Job (13:24; 16:9; 33:10) to indicate the enmity between Job and God. According to Samuel, Yahweh himself became an adversary (satan) to Saul (I Sam. 28:16), and Yahweh is credited with raising up adversaries in the form of rebels against the reign of Solomon (I Kings 11:14, 23).

When Balaam set out on an unfriendly mission against Israel astride his faithful ass, the angel of Yahweh blocked the way three times. First the ass shied into a field, then he crushed Balaam's foot against the wall, and finally he balked and lay down on the trail. Then Balaam belabored the animal with his staff until the ass found a voice and talked back to him. This opened the eyes of the Seer, and he saw the angel of Yahweh with a drawn sword before him, "And the angel of the Lord said to him, 'Why have you struck your ass these three times? Behold, I have come forth to withstand you (the old version, "for an adversary," or satan) because your way is perverse before me'" (Num. 22:32).

In Psalm 109:6 we have a passage with this word in which it is not quite clear whether the poet is talking about a tribunal set up in heaven or on earth, and the difference determines whether we say, "Let Satan"—(as in the King James Version)—or, "let an accuser bring him to trial" (as in the Revised Standard Version).

In two other places only in the Old Testament, besides the prologue of Job, Satan appears as a supernatural individual. In Zechariah 3:1-2, the word "satan" is used twice, first as a title and then as a common noun. Joshua the high priest is standing before the angel of Yahweh, clothed in filthy rags, symbolizing the hardships of the people. The Satan stands at his right hand "to be his adversary (satan)." And The Satan is rebuked by Yahweh for his opposition to this "brand plucked out of the fire." Here, as in Job, The Satan appears to be an official title.

In I Chronicles 21:1, Satan appears as a proper name without the definite article. It is an episode in the career of David, a census which was interpreted as a sin and the cause of a pestilence. In the earlier version (II Sam. 24:1) it is said that the anger of Yahweh was kindled against Israel and moved David to the deed. But in the account of the Chronicler it is Satan who stood up against Israel and inspired David. This change in the interpretation of the same event shows the change which took place in Jewish thought about God after the Exile. One might say that the explanation of ultimate causes of evil became more profound as the view of Satan became more advanced.

Thus Job's Satan appears in the midst of an ancient culture in which the concept of the grand devil is slowly taking form. He is not yet the devil tempter of the New Testament, nor the prince of angels fallen from heaven to become ruler of the kingdoms of this world, as in the apocalyptic tradition. He is still among the sons of God in the councils of heaven. His activity is entirely subject to divine permission. He has a function, as pointed out by many commentators, not unlike that of the Advocatus Diaboli in the Roman Catholic Curia of the Vatican, whose business it is to search out all the evil which may in any way discredit a candidate for canonization as a saint. Satan travels about and up and down in the earth in search of impiety and hypocrisy among the sons of men, having a special eye to prosperous Semites, among whom parsimony is reputed to be a very ancient sin, and who have the persistent belief that prosperity is a badge of goodness and the special mark of divine favor. When specifically delegated by the Almighty, Satan has the power to test the sincerity of men by affliction and adversity, and thus to see whether they "fear God for nought." But the power is strictly limited. When Yahweh builds a fence around a man, Satan cannot break through until the divine permission is secured.

In the story of Zechariah, Satan is rebuked for his delight in the filthy rags of Joshua, and a reward is ordered for the faithful high priest. But on the other hand, perhaps it is not right, certainly not the way of the world, for a saint to enjoy nothing but good and prosperity. Most of the saints have been made that way by suffering. So Yahweh himself puts Satan on the scent of Job through a banter: "Have you considered my servant Job, that there is none like him on the earth, a blameless and upright man, who fears God and turns away from evil."

Such a boast would indicate that the Lord has some lurking uncertainty. This is the first man since the fall of Adam to receive such high praise. Does it all mark a contest between Yahweh and Satan over the question of moral perfection? The Almighty has risked everything in making this creature and endowing him with freedom. It would be the highest achievement of divine creative wisdom to evolve a perfect and upright man in the scheme of things. The highest of the divine purposes are at stake in this contest. Adam, first, and then Job, puts the design of God to the test. Adam failed; Job has the advantage of history.

Satan is the cynic; hedge man about with every protection from evil, and reward him freely with every pleasure and happiness, and, to be sure, he will be pious and keep the law. Put him on the rack and he will soon crack up. Let Satan at him and see how long he will maintain his piety! Yahweh has to yield. To refuse would show that his zeal to create the perfect example leads him to play favorites. So the satanic fury is turned loose and destroys both Job's prosperity and his posterity.

But Satan cannot touch Job's integrity; he stands the test. Yet the cynicism of Satan knows no bounds. Job's skin is still intact, and his wife and friends pity him. "Skin for skin! All that a man has he will give for his life." Once a contest of this sort is started, there is no point in stopping until the last pound of flesh has been exacted. Yahweh must yield again, and the hand of Satan is laid against Job's person. The pity of wife and friends is turned into fearsome accusation. Job is reduced to the necessity of pure faith; all the props are gone. Does he stand this test? That depends on the point of view with which the whole poem is judged. The veil of heaven was not pulled back again for us to see how it stood when Satan returned to collect his wager. There is only a dim clue in those words of commendation for Job and condemnation for his friends in the epilogue (42:7-9).

Meaning of the Satan Episode

What can be the purpose of such an episode in the book? Aside from the sheer dramatic force of the scene itself, two suggestions are usually gleaned from it by the interpreters: First, it forever sets the mark of satanic scorn upon "a religion of barter." Ralph Tyler Flewelling in his *Christ and the Dramas of Doubt* sees this challenge of Satan as setting the stage for that orthodox notion with which the three friends afflict Job so sorely and which he repudiates so fearlessly in the debate, namely, that piety guarantees prosperity and is evidenced by it. Satan's sneer, "Does Job fear God for nought?" has certainly had the effect of lifting faith in God to a higher level than the religion of prosperity. Satan is capable of appreciating sincerity, and his scorn at the absence of it is only the judgment of the Lord himself against all such.

Secondly, popular interpretations of the book also find in

the Satan story a heavenly insight into a mysterious purpose in innocent suffering. Sinners suffer as punishment for their sins, but saints suffer by the design of an inscrutable providence to test the quality of their righteousness. We may repudiate it with much feeling when it is in the mouth of such strangers to suffering as Eliphaz, but when the heroes of suffering like St. Francis of Assisi apply it to themselves, it becomes a beautiful doctrine. (This will be the subject of treatment later. Here we are concerned more directly with the character and role of Satan.)

Certainly this is not an attractive picture of the old tribal deity of Israel, getting a faithful servant into trouble with Satan by what appears on the surface as just an idle boast, and then yielding in the spirit of a wager to the cruel test. This must have been one of the passages which led a man like Marcion, the greatest of the Gnostics, in the second century A.D., to reject entirely the Old Testament God. Yahweh, he taught, is the creator of the world and its ruler in cruel justice, identical with the principalities and powers against which the kingdom of heaven must struggle, according to St. Paul, and in no way related to the God of Love whom Jesus revealed. The common basis for the Gnostic heresies is known as "dualism." In effect, they argued that man is confronted by two deities, one evil and the other good, one the ruler of the world of material things, the other the ruler of the realm of spirit.

Dualism as an answer to the problem of evil has had such a powerful hold upon the imagination that it needs to be examined, even though it cannot be ascribed to our Job poet. Not so very long after the book was written, Satan came to stand for that other kingdom of evil in opposition to God and the good. The Job prologue, therefore, is in a transition period. In it we find only a provisional dualism. Satan is in no sense an independent cause of evil; he acts always as an agent of God and in the end accomplishes purposes which are

included in divine providence. This is in strict keeping with
the spirit of nearly all the canonical scriptures of the Old
Testament. In the midst of an almost universal polytheism
and polydemonism it is nothing short of remarkable that
Hebrew faith remained so thoroughgoing and constant in its
monotheism. Yahweh is held to be the source of evil as well
as of good. There are demonic powers, but they are strictly
accountable to him. The references to Rahab and Leviathan,
which are identifiable with Babylonian chaos monsters, as indicated in the last chapter, show that the Jews recognized a
demonic element in the cosmos, but Tiamat has been overcome and stricken through in the act of creation, and Leviathan is now the plaything of God.

Theologians, like the Job poets, maintained this strict
monotheism, but the flash views of Satan in Job, Zechariah,
and Chronicles show that dualism was creeping into popular
thought after the Exile. The ideal of Yahweh was gradually
moralized so that it became increasingly difficult to assign
evil directly to him as in primitive Hebrew thought. As the
German commentator, Duhm, puts it, they "ascribed incon-
ceivably heavy blows, from which no bravery and no foresight
can protect, to a hostile higher creature, . . . a kind of official
spy and public prosecutor."[1] Such blows are those which
befell the Jerusalem community when Joshua was high priest,
shortly after the return from Babylonia, symbolized by the
rags in which he stands before Yahweh in Zechariah 3:1-2.
In Job, such blows fall on an individual. And with this
change God became increasingly remote and transcendent,
so that angels came to figure more and more in the good
offices of providence. By the time of the Book of Daniel,
God manifests himself not at all, but angels and demons

[1] D. Bernhard Duhm, *Das Buch Hiob* (Freiburg: Mohr Verlag, 1897).
The quotation is a translation of the German text. Duhm regards the whole
Satan idea as "the personification of the whims of fate which one cannot
escape because one is never secure from mistakes, especially the unconscious
ones."

abound. Such dualism came to full flower in the apocalyptic world view which arose to dominate Jewish thought in the period between the Testaments and which became the basis of the New Testament world view. Arising out of Persia, this more hopeless dualism settled on the Biblical world so completely that the provisional dualism of the Old Testament passed under a cloud from which it did not emerge again to clear expression until the rise of modern scientific monism.

Satan and dualism cannot be dismissed as a solution of the problem of evil simply by saying that there is none of it in the earlier Biblical literature. The Satan in Job cannot be set aside so easily as saying that there is no Satan in the dialogue argument of the book. The devil too deeply matches some needs of the human spirit, both logical and psychological.

Origin of Demons

Demons have their origin, according to the most widely held theory, in the primitive animistic tendency of man to personify the terrifying forces against which he must contend. Here is a statement of the idea from a standard French work on *The Devil:*

> Before being a religious animal, man was a fearful animal. For thousands of years, knowing nothing of the phenomena of nature, impotent to protect himself against storms and catastrophes of every kind, or even against the beasts, incapable of perceiving the reasons and the causes of those wondrous happenings which could not fail to sow terror, he was unable to discover whether or not the volitional element existed in external objects. Therefore, projecting outside himself wills which he believed were being exercised upon him, he peopled the world about him, in his first imaginative effort, with lives, opinions, and passions like his own.[2]

Primitive man responded to these personified forces in two different ways, and the difference marks the basic distinction

[2] M. Garçon and J. Vinchon, *The Devil*, translated by S. H. Guest (New York: E. P. Dutton & Co., 1930), p. 10. Quoted by permission.

between magic and religion. In his efforts to understand and manipulate such powers to his own ends, he develops the incantations of magic. In his efforts to understand them and conform to their demands as the end of life, he is religious. The line between the two is not always sharply drawn. The Hebrews very early developed such a strong religious attachment and adjustment to their tribal deity, Yahweh, that they lost in a remarkable degree the primitive polytheism and demonology and became generally hostile to the practices of magic; so much so that when Satan finally appears among them, he becomes not a being to be propitiated by incantations but avoided and opposed on the field of moral battle. And in the Hebrew-Christian tradition, all employment of the magical arts has been interpreted, by the orthodox tradition, as a league with Satan.

Then there must be recognized a deeper-rooted psychological motive for demons, like Satan: such is the tendency of the human mind to project and objectify the struggle of the inner life. The battling demons of nature are always connected in many subtle ways with the devils that haunt dreams and tempt the soul into forbidden paths. Personality must be won through conflict, and devils and demons have from early times been the means for unifying and objectifying the enemy in the struggle. Demon possession satisfied the need for an ancient explanation of abnormal people, and modern science has not radically changed the picture; it only supplied the ancient devils with new names, the class terms of psychology and biology: repressions, complexes, libido and biological ancestry. But their countenances are not much changed.

Natural sciences have put many events on an impersonal basis of understanding and adjustment. When a modern city is shaken down by an earthquake, we no longer lay it to an earth demon or thundering Zeus trying to vent his wrath on sinful man. Japanese mythology is more impersonal in the explanation that a giant catfish lies under that oft-quaking land and occasionally must shift its position. This is doubtless a playful suggestion and indicates that among that stoical people primitive fears had been so far conquered. Geologists explain that adjustments of the earth crust along fault lines now partly charted are necessary to relieve the strains occasioned by cooling and volcanic stresses. Physicists have studied the phenomena in relation to the earth's magnetism. And when one contemplates the terrific whirl of the earth through space it is easy to speculate about the imbalance of centripetal and centrifugal forces. Whatever explanation is given to such events, they mean, both to the scientists and to common folk, that the forces operative take no notice of puny man in the crash. This tendency of modern thought to depersonalize all the agencies which affect the hapless lot of a Job or a citizen of a democracy in the atomic age does not settle the problem of evil. The result seems to be either a hopeless pessimism, on the one hand, or on the other a very unrealistic view of the demonic and irrational existence into which man is cast. Dualism, therefore, has its rationale even in our day.

Hopeless Dualism

We need to make more explicit the distinction we are suggesting between a provisional and a hopeless dualism. The Satan idea of the Old Testament is a provisional dualism because it is developed within a strict monotheism in which God determines the moral order of the universe. He is creator and ruler and ultimately responsible for both good and bad. Devils, no more than evil human beings, can exist in irreconcilable opposition to the good. They have a provisional status, but ultimately they serve the divine purposes. The two best examples of provisional devils are the Satan of Job and the Mephistopheles of Goethe's *Faust*.

Any system in which the evil principle is personified and set in eternal and irredeemable opposition to the good is a hopeless dualism. Evil is hopeless only where it is metaphysical, that is, concrete and personalized, as in the traditional Christian concept of Satan generated in the Middle Ages, and presented in its most dramatic form by Dante's *Divine Comedy*, and in its most majestic form by Milton's *Paradise Lost*. According to this, we should not class as hopeless those dualistic philosophies in which the evil principle is merely an abstraction, as in the Platonic tradition, to be purged by the refining fires, leaving only the good as permanent.

Hopeless dualism need be pessimistic only about the destiny of evil persons. It does not imply a complete pessimism; in fact, it may be supremely optimistic about the kingdom of the good. Every religious system has its way of escape from evil and the doom of evil. Demons are subdued or controlled in three different ways, dependent upon the cultural level of the sect: exorcism, by which they are outwitted and rendered impotent—the medicine man must be more clever than the spirits; propitiation, by which the aroused wrath of the demons is appeased. Sacrificial rites, as in Homer, are necessary to secure either the help of friendly gods or to avoid the wrath of hostile or indifferent deities. From the early Christian point of view, these gods are demons. In the Middle Ages an artist charged with painting a portrait of the devil had to take certain magical precautions and then be very cautious with the likeness that he did not incur the wrath of Satan.[3] The third way, represented in all ethical religions, is to overcome evil with good works, as in the teachings of St. Paul (Romans 12:21).

Some practical ways in which such a dualism affects our faith and practice may be observed. Modern enthusiasm in preaching the millennial doctrine and a catastrophic end of the age often leads to the drawing from Scriptures rather ex-

[3] M. Rudin, *The Devil in Legend and Literature* (Chicago: Open Court Publishing Co., 1931), p. 37.

act predictions about the time of the end and the number of the saved. The number is always very small compared with the multitudes who have lived under the sun. It is perhaps typical of dualists—or is it just the colossal conceit of the Old Adam within us?—that such preachers always number themselves among the saved. Some of the earlier Calvinists are reputed to have attained that state of renunciation in which they were "willing to be damned for the glory of God," but they made themselves famous for good works and piety by trying "to make their calling and election sure." To imagine someone else damned is one way to make one feel more sure of one's own salvation, and such is the compensation offered by dualism.

Such a dualism also has a kind of optimism about the good which makes a poem like Job impossible. If we can assign the causes of evil to some vile brood of demons, as is done in the Persian religion, then the problem of Job does not arise. The goodness of Yahweh would be assumed, and the time of the prophets would be employed, like Zarathustra, in fighting khafstras (bad animals), and like him, the poets would end their writing career with a few hymns to the god of light and moral sayings to the faithful. Yet we must acknowledge that one of the great poems of all time, the *Divine Comedy*, was produced in the literary mill of medieval dualism, and the *Inferno* is about as hopeless as could be conceived. Yet Dante never faces the problem of Job, the question of unexplained suffering in this life. The scene of the *Comedy* is laid in the life beyond, and Christian theology by that time had settled the problem—for the medieval mind at least—with the concepts of hell, purgatory, and heaven, in which the governmental theory of divine justice is worked out. Every soul gets an ultimate reward in terms of exact merit.

Persian Dualism

The fountainhead of dualism for all the religions of the Near East is the Zoroastrian religion of ancient Persia, a small remnant of which survives among the Parsees of modern India. One of their sacred books, the Zend-Avesta, preserved the early faith. The Gathas or psalms of this work are thought to be the oldest section and to be the work of Zarathustra himself, in part at least. He was a reformer of the seventh century B.C. who founded the system in ancient Iran. The achievement of this prophet was the systematic reorganization of the theology of the older Aryan religion with its chaotic pantheon of nature deities. Hesiod, a Greek poet of about the same time, undertook a similar renovation of the ancient Greek mythology in his *Theogony*, and the principle which he followed in laying the foundation for monotheism in pagan culture was a family relationship among the gods. The principle of Zarathustra was more radical; it was ethical. The Aryan deities are classified in the *Avesta* as good or bad, according to whether the power of each is helpful or inimical to the ends of human life, and this ethical dualism becomes the organizing principle not only for theology but for the whole of life.

There are two primal powers struggling against each other in the universe. One is the god of light, Ahura Mazda, around whom are ranged all the forces of the cosmos and those in human society which stand for light, truth, goodness, and joy. The old nature gods who represent the friendly forces of the world are assigned to places as attributes, messengers, and subrulers. All friendly animals and good men are the creation and agents of Mazda. Over against this realm is that commanded by the demon of darkness, Angra Mainyu, also called Ahriman. Around him are ranged all the powers of evil, suffering, terror, lying, and death, both in the cosmos and in the sphere of human action. The old gods who represent the ter-

rifying aspects of nature are subordinated to and obedient to
Ahriman, as are also all useless or vicious animals and bad
men. Here is a sample of the songs as translated in the *Sacred
Books of the East.*

> Thus are the primeval spirits who, as a pair combining their
> opposite strivings, and yet each independent in his action, have
> been famed of old. They are a better thing, they too, and a
> worse, as to thought, as to word, and as to deed. And between
> these two let the wisely acting choose aright. Choose ye not as
> the evildoers! (*Yasna XXX*, S.B.E., Vol. XXXI)

> Yea, I will declare the world's two first spirits, of whom the
> more bountiful thus spake to the harmful: Neither our thoughts,
> nor commands, nor our understandings, nor our beliefs, nor
> our deeds, nor our consciences, nor our souls, are at one.
>   (*Yasna XLV*)

Coming together in a clash from the first, the two primeval
spirits create life and death and order the destiny of the
world. The abstractness and simplicity of the early poems
receive ample elaboration and imaginative decoration in the
later documents of the Avesta. All creation is a battlefield,
and all creatures are ranged in the fight; there is no neutrality
or no man's land. There is no earthly paradise, no Garden of
Eden. Life is a warfare. Man must choose his master and
gird himself for the battle against evil, ignorance, death, disintegration. There is no release during life; no escape into
some other-worldly realm this side of death. There are no
monasteries or banyan forests in ancient Iran. Zarathustra is
no pale-faced ascetic, seeking to overcome evil by negations,
as though evil itself were a mere negation. All the natural
processes which make for health and happiness are ennobled
by him. Truth, beauty, goodness, and gladness are the ends
of life; but they are to be won only by the faithful and cour-
ageous fighter. More corn must be planted, evil men destroyed, khafstras exterminated, lawlessness suppressed, and
children begotten. "He who sows corn, sows holiness."

O Maker of the material world, thou Holy One!
Which is the second place where the Earth feels most happy?
Ahura Mazda answered: "It is the place whereon one of the
    faithful
erects a house with a priest within, with cattle, with a wife,
with children, and good herds within: and wherein afterwards
the cattle go on thriving, holiness is thriving, fodder is thriving,
the dog is thriving, the wife is thriving, the child is thriving,
the fire is thriving, and every blessing of life is thriving."
                              (Vendidad, S.B.E., Vol. IV)

The faith of Zarathustra became the spiritual dynamic of
the Old Persian Empire which conquered Babylonia and
spread across the Eastern world in the conquests of Cyrus.
Exiled Jews in Babylon must have found much in common
with the worship of Ahura Mazda, and they were doubtless
a valuable fifth column for Cyrus beside the river Chebar, for
under his patronage the remnant returned and established
anew the Judaic faith in Palestine. The writer of Second
Isaiah certainly had this dualism in mind when he penned
his oracles. He wrote a paean to Cyrus which hails the con-
queror as the Anointed of Yahweh, and then proceeds as follows:

> I am the LORD, and there is no other,
>   besides me there is no God;
>   I gird you, though you do not know me,
> that men may know, from the rising of the sun
>   and from the west, that there is none besides me;
>   I am the LORD, and there is no other.
> I form light and create darkness,   ·
>   I make weal and create woe,
>   I am the LORD, who do all these things. (Isa. 45:5-7)

This is a stout reaffirmation of the ancient Hebrew faith in
the face of a powerful influence, if not a threat, from dualism.
In subsequent years there are many crosscurrents of influence
between Palestine and Persia. After a century or more, a
strongly Persian type of dualism gradually emerged in Jewish
apocalypticism. Angels and demons began to take over more

functions in the affairs of this world. But there is very little parallel between Satan and Ahriman. Satan is a Hebrew-Christian devil pure and simple. His origin is in the Jewish theology and its struggle with the problem of evil in its own poetic way. His growth and epic stature in the Western world would have been impossible except for the nurturing soil of Christian faith and piety.

The religion of Zarathustra passed through elaborate developments. During the period of the Sassanid Dynasty, in the third to seventh centuries A.D., a sort of new testament known as the Pahlavi Texts was added to the Zend-Avesta. Here we see a development which in many ways parallels the Jewish and Christian apocalyptic tradition and was probably greatly influenced by that.

An early legend promised the faithful devotees of the Avesta the miraculous advent of a savior, Saoshyant, the Fiend Smiter, one who will put an end to the struggle which was so real to the sage of Iran. A holy maid shall bathe in the lake Kasava and receive the seed of the Holy Zarathustra, miraculously preserved there, and the son to be born shall be "a friend of Ahura Mazda, knowing the victorious knowledge." He shall restore the earth and bring life and immortality, "and the Drug shall perish, though she may rush on every side to kill the holy beings." This legend develops into a full-fledged eschatology in the Pahlavi Texts, with a detailed picture of a millennium, a physical resurrection, a final judgment, and a great renovation of the universe in which even hell shall be cleaned out and purified. Late Zoroastrianism, therefore, takes on a paler complexion than the dark and hopeless dualism of the Avesta.

Chapter 5

THE CHRISTIAN DEVIL

Whatever influences may have emanated from Eastern dualism, the Satan which came to occupy a central place in Christian mythology achieves a stature and uniqueness unmatched by any other devil. He is The Satan of Job and the other Old Testament writers developed into a figure of epic and sometimes tragic proportions. Ahriman is a dark shadow across the landscape of the East. Satan is a cosmic person, concrete, dramatic, whose hand is in every catastrophe, whose guile is in every temptation, whose leer is in every failure. Late Jewish apocalypticism transmitted this devil to the New Testament and Christian thought, but he did not attain full eminence until Christian theology had reached its zenith. It takes a profound theology to create a magnificent rebel. Everything which God and Christ are not, the complete foil, such is the medieval Satan.

The influence of Persian dualism is most directly seen in Gnostic heresies and especially in Manicheism, which flourished in the Christian era and rivaled the Church until the fall of the empire. The orthodox theology of the Church Fathers was developed in opposition to them. But in none of these is the demonic realm personified and concrete. Evil is an abstraction, identified in various ways with things, with darkness or with materiality, with the flesh as opposed to the spirit. All such doctrines became heresies for the simple reason that Christianity developed first of all a dogma of creation out of nothing. Things, therefore, are not in themselves evil, neither the flesh nor the material substance, not even darkness. Even the demons exist by divine fiat and permission, as in the case of Job's Satan. St. Paul says that God through the Son is the creator even of the "principalities and powers" (Col. 1:16), by which he means the kingdom of devils. Orthodox Christians have never forgotten this, and even in times when the works of Satan have been most vivid and vicious, care has been exercised to say that divine permission alone makes them possible. The works of the flesh, the deeds done in darkness, are evil because of wills in rebellion. The devil and bad men love darkness because their deeds are evil, and often they work through the realm of material things. The man of God must cultivate the spirit, but when this means abuse of the flesh or rejection of material objects as such, as in extreme forms of asceticism, he skirts the borders of heresy.

Apocalyptic Dualism

Apocalyptic dualism in Palestine was much more than an imitation of foreign philosophy; it was the indigenous development of the prophetic spirit in the face of entirely new and trying circumstances. The long delayed consummation of Israel's history, and centuries of intense suffering on the part of the faithful, put a great strain upon the early faith in the nearness of Yahweh and his responsibility for good or evil. The heart-rending cry of Second Esdras shows the need of the Jew in the Greek period for a theodicy:

> Are the deeds of Babylon better than those of Sion? Or is there any other nation that knoweth thee beside Israel? or what tribes have so believed thy covenants as these tribes of Jacob? And yet their reward appeareth not, and their labour hath no fruit: for I have gone hither and thither through the nations, and I see that they abound in wealth, and think not upon thy commandments. . . . Thou shalt find that men who may be reckoned by name have kept thy precepts; but nations thou shalt not find. (Chapter 3)

Uriel appears to answer his question, but it is a series of eva-
sive oracles which have the import that God, at times hidden
in his own providence, will bring the wicked to destruction
and the righteous to salvation. In the meantime, wickedness
must increase. Then the Book of Daniel draws a sharp line
of distinction between a world order in the grip of powers
utterly hostile to God and the transcendent divine order; and
the faithful are warned not to expect anything but tribulation
until the time when the angel Michael shall stand up as a
divine champion to usher in a new age.

In the Book of Jubilees (ca. 100 B.C.), Satan still comes
into the counsels of heaven. The story deals with the grand-
sons of Noah after the Flood, and they are still plagued with
evil spirits. Noah makes an eloquent prayer that the demons
shall be destroyed, else again they corrupt the human family,
and the LORD decides to consign them to the pit; but Satan
stands up with a vigorous plea:

> If some of them are not left to me, I shall not be able to
> execute the power of my will on the sons of men; for these are
> for corruption and leading astray before my judgment, for great
> is the wickedness of the sons of men. (10:8)

And Satan got his way with the Lord again for "a tenth part
of them were left that they might be subject before Satan on
the earth."

Two books which are thought to have been written in the
century of 50 B.C. to 50 A.D., the Ethiopic Book of Enoch
and the Slavonic Book of the Secrets of Enoch, appear to be
the earliest sources of several basic ideas which came into
Christian demonology and eschatology. In both books a rebellion takes place in heaven and Satan is cast down to earth
with his satans. There he enters the Garden of Eden and
deceives Eve because of his jealousy toward Adam in ruling
the earth. (There is no mention yet of turning into a serpent.) The satans look upon the daughters of men and see
that they are fair, and seduce them, thereby spreading evil in

the world. But according to the Ethiopic Book, man is ruined because he learns the secrets of the angels and the violence of the satans. One of the devils taught him the secrets of wisdom and

> instructed mankind in writing with ink and paper, and thereby many sinned. . . . For men were not created for such a purpose, to give confirmation to their faith with pen and ink. For men were created exactly like the angels, to the intent that they should continue pure and righteous. (LXIX)

Earthly existence is in the grip of satanic powers from which the faithful will be rescued by a Messianic intervention. Here is the earliest statement in surviving literature of the idea of a general resurrection for Israel, and the Hebrew Sheol is turned into fiery Gehenna, a place for final punishment of wicked men and satans.

In the Slavonic version, Enoch is transported through the heavens to the seventh where he stands before the Lord who explains creation and the fall of Satan. Originally he was Satanail, one of the archangels, who

> entertained an impossible idea, that he should make his throne higher than the clouds over the earth, and should be equal in rank to My power. And I hurled him from the heights with his angels. And he was flying in the air continually, above the abyss. (XXIX)

Here is the explanation of St. Paul's phrase, "prince of the power of the air" (Eph. 2:2). In the second heaven, Enoch finds the rebellious angels waiting in utter gloom for their day of retribution. In the third level he passes through the beautiful Garden of Paradise prepared for the righteous, and then at the northern extremity he is shown the place of punishment, a hell of fire and ice guarded by angels, terrible and without pity. The idea of several such heavens had a short but uncertain reception among the Christian Fathers, but it faded after it was purged of the notion that Satan has access to heaven and that hell is located there. Here also seems to be the earliest source of the millennium doctrine, although the passage is obscure. Time is reckoned on the pattern of the seven days of creation, each day a thousand years. The seventh millennium is the divine Sabbath, and on the turn of the eighth comes the end of time.

Satan, Christ, and Lucifer

Religious thought in the New Testament, of course, goes far beyond this apocalypticism, but in world view and philosophy of history there is little added. While Satan and the demons are never given the clear delineation which they acquired in subsequent Christian literature, they have a significant role. Satan is named thirty-five times, and thirty-seven times he is called the devil, "diabolos," seven times Beelzebub. Demons and devils are mentioned numerous times. The multiplication from the Old Testament is very significant. Most of these passages ascribe certain events to diabolic agency or describe qualities which belong to Satan. He is a deceiver, father of lies, tempter; he will take advantage of weakness, he knows and perverts Scripture, and he loves to pose as an angel of light.

Only once does Satan appear as a person, and that is in a passage to put beside the prologue to the Book of Job as decisive in forming the Christian concept. Satan confronts Jesus as the tempter in the wilderness. And a very different being he is from the spirit which plagued the patriarch. No longer is he in the counsels of heaven to castigate pious hypocrisy; he is the sworn enemy of the Son of God. Christ says (Luke 10:18) that he "saw Satan fall like lightning from heaven." That must have been when he was with the Father at the beginning of time. But now Satan is the prince and god of this world (John 14:30; II Cor. 4:4); all its glory and power are at his disposal, an authority which he confesses to be derived from the higher source (Luke 4:6). He has still his cosmic powers so that he can appear out of nowhere, and he has miraculous facility at transportation; he can whisk Jesus off to the high mountain or set him on the pinnacle of the Temple—powers which came to figure greatly in medieval notions of the activities of Satan. The Christ, on the other hand, is now Jesus of Nazareth, a human being, who is hungry after a forty-day fast and puzzled about his destiny in the affairs of men. Satan's weapon here is not to unloose the violence of nature upon man but to make a subtle appeal to the basic weaknesses of the human heart in the effort to seduce him into the ways of sin. Job's Satan is a nature demon, purely; the Christian devil is a moral rebel. In the New Testament he figures chiefly as the cunning tempter, although suffering and disease are regarded as the direct work of demons connected with the satanic rule of the natural order. Satan is still the cynic; he does not himself change the stone to bread in order to demonstrate his powers to Jesus; he challenges the powers of the Son of God.

The final touch of Scripture is the fearful judgment passed upon Satan in the Book of Revelation:

> And the devil who had deceived them was thrown into the lake of fire and brimstone where the beast and the false prophet were, and they will be tormented day and night for ever and ever. (20:10)

But the picture of Christian dualism is not complete until Satan has been identified with the archangel light-bearer, Lucifer. The pattern was prepared in the story of a rebellion in heaven and given its Biblical formulation in the Apocalypse of St. John (Rev. 9:1; 12:7-12): Satan and his minions battling with Michael and the angels for control of heaven; Satan defeated and cast headlong, falling like a star to earth, and the keys of the pit delivered unto him. But Lucifer is not in the Biblical account; in fact, the word is actually applied to Christ in the Vulgate Version of II Peter 1:19, where it is a Latin translation of the same Greek word which is used for Lucifer in the Septuagint Version of Isaiah 14:12. In English it is rendered "daystar."

The earliest record we have been able to find for the identification of Satan with Lucifer is in Origen's *De Principiis, v.* The Satan which Christ saw falling as lightning from heaven (Luke 10:18) Origen identifies with Isaiah's Lucifer, and it is obvious that he has a theoretical reason for doing so. Origen is at pains to deny one of the notions of the current Gnostic dualism that Satan is the ancient demon of darkness (Ahriman). He is expounding the doctrine of the fall. Satan now is the ruler of darkness—not darkness itself—but originally he was Lucifer, one of the bright lights of the heavenly constellation. His place in the abyss comes about from the fall described by the prophet Isaiah (14:12-20). Origen may have had some apocalyptic source now lost, but it may also be a fair sample of the unhistorical allegorizing common to some of the Church Fathers.

Historically, Lucifer in the oracle of Isaiah is a symbol for the Babylonian king who sought to exalt himself to heaven and came down with an awful crash. But Lucifer, for Christians, will always mean the archangel, one of the brightest luminaries of heaven, who rebelled through pride and arrogance against the rule of the one true God, and after a battle was pitched over the battlements to fall into the pit where he reigns forever as Satan. From there he has access to earth. At the beginning of sacred history, he sneaked into the Garden of Eden, changed himself into a serpent, and achieved the seduction of Eve and the fall of man. With this the myth of Satanism is complete. It received its authoritative formulation in the eleventh century with the circulation of St. Anselm's *Dialogus de casu diaboli.*

The fall of Satan and the fall of Adam, put together, formulate the mythos of the origin of evil. Christian theologians have always insisted that sin belongs to the freedom of man alone, but they put a very heavy burden on such a frail instrument. Even for the strict rationalists it has its paradoxical aspect. Puny man was caught in some powerful forces. God was in the Garden with a thundering prohibition, a psychological problem in itself; and a snake was in the grass with cunning deceit, because a prior rebellion among the spirits had already taken place.

The Medieval Devil

One who digs into the great theological works of the Fathers and the Middle Ages finds them remarkably free from demonolatry. The most curious relic of Satanism there is the ransom theory of the atonement. It may be found as early as the writings of Irenaeus and it was given rather undogmatic credence by St. Augustine. The doctrine was based on the belief that Satan as ruler of this world holds all souls under bondage, and having failed in the attempt to seduce the Son of God by temptations, he required the latter's blood as a ransom from God for all other souls. The blood of Christ shed on Calvary became the redemption price paid to the devil for man's salvation. This doctrine was not replaced until the eleventh century, and again by that definitive thinker, St. Anselm. He substituted the doctrine of the "substitutionary atonement." Man's sin is an infinite affront to the divine majesty, requiring an infinite sacrifice for propitiation, which man himself cannot provide. The infinite Son of God is the substitute. Actually, Satan is replaced in the picture by a monotheistic Judge who rules both heaven and earth by an abstract justice. But "substitute" is not nearly so poetic a word as "ransom," so it is the latter which clings in hymnology if not in theology.

For sheer hideousness no picture of Satan is quite the equal of Dante's Lucifer, frozen in the ice at the center of the ninth circle of the Inferno. "To describe the bottom of the universe is not an enterprise," says Dante, "for a tongue that cries mamma and papa." In the fall from heaven, Satan has plowed through the earth to the center, which is the bottom of hell, half on one side of an ice barrier and half on the other. Great batlike wings ceaselessly fan the air into a gale up through the caverns of the damned. His head presents three ogre faces, dripping with tears and blood, representing a satanic trinity of hatred, impotence, and ignorance. Being a rebel himself, he has landed in the place of torment for all traitors; so while the eternal ice gnaws at his groin, he chews on Judas Iscariot in one mouth and on Brutus and Cassius in the other two. The artistic portrayal of the supremely ugly is complete, but, aside from this, the conception is disappointing. Satan is not the architect of hell or even its ruler. God is both of these, and all the supernal bliss of the *Paradiso* can hardly resolve the question of why a good God should design such a place and the creatures to inhabit it. There is a rich range of moral insight in the comments which Dante makes on the characters which he finds in the shades, yet it can hardly be said that he actually confronts the tragic situation of man in real life. Satan is roaming the earth; he is not frozen in hell.

In popular folklore, the Christian devil acquired his full stature. Two factors contributed to his eminence and personification. First is the fact that in the ancient history of religions no new faith ever actually exterminated the gods opposed; they survived in the superstitious fears of the people. Second, the stronger the official opposition became to Satan and his kingdom, the clearer became his reality. So the Biblical Satan was invested with all the characteristics condemned in rival pagan deities of Europe. Satyr and nymph, naiad and dryad, kelpie and nixie, daeva and jinn, wraith and hobgoblin, all combine their picturesque qualities with such ugly and vicious ancient demons as Moloch, Beelzebub, and

Belial to make the devil and his kingdom what they became for our forefathers.

Satanism and Revolt

The story of medieval witchcraft is often mentioned but seldom told in clear terms, for it is a complicated and cloudy picture. The author of Job has surely had many an immortal shiver at what finally happened to his poetic Satan. It is a tale of horror. Recent historians recognize it as an institution of revolt against totalitarian ideology. In the rising tide of revolt against feudal culture and Catholic theology after the thirteenth century, the devil often took on the form of champion of the oppressed, a rebel leader of rebels. Heresy is always a normal expression of feeling in minority groups. The doctors of the Inquisition often had great difficulty in distinguishing witchcraft from heresy, although the matter was not decisive, for the penalty was the same in either case— death at the stake.

It is not surprising that Protestant sectarians were associated with the sons of Belial, because when orthodoxy assumes the infallibility of its position, all else must belong to the kingdom of Satan. But turning to the records of the Protestant side, we find that Satan was never in concert with the Reformers. Yet he was very real to them, and always, in some mysterious way, in league with the powers ruling in Rome. There doubtless was never a more genuine devil than the one which gave Martin Luther the leer of discouragement from behind his stove in the Wartburg as he strove with the Scriptures, trying to "make God talk Deutsch." [1] Where the

---

[1] The authenticity of the story should be doubted, to be sure. It is typical of the sort of devil legend which clustered about famous men in those days. When Luther started on his famous trip to Worms, he declared that he would go and face the Papal Legate even if a devil lurked under every roof tile, but Luther made no mistake about who the devils were that he had to confront. See D'Aubigne's *History of the Reformation in the Sixteenth Century* (New York: John B. Alden, 1883), Book IX, Chap. v.

devil's accomplices lie depends on which side of the argument we happen to be.

Witchcraft, in these centuries, was a sort of third center of belief and practice, outside the Church and outside the reforming sects, but cutting across the line of both and centering in the vast Promethean mass struggling to rise in European culture, what we have come to call "the proletariat." This, too, was a religion, but its roots were deeper in the primitive libido than the rationalism which produced Scholasticism. Demonolatry attained the status of an underworld institution, and at times certainly became a formidable threat, as much to Protestants as to Catholics, as may be seen in Luther's reaction to the Peasants' Revolt in Germany or the campaign against witchcraft in England, which probably attained its greatest ferocity during Cromwell's Protectorate.

The amazing thing is that the Church had nothing better to offer than a countersystem of exorcism and sacred amulets, and a threat of torture, fire, and the gibbet. The most important document of the Church's campaign against witchcraft is now available to English readers, and it has the greatest interest for the historical scholar, the *Malleus Maleficarum*, first published at Cologne in 1489.[2] In 1484 Pope Innocent VIII issued a bull, *Summis desiderantes affectibus*, which outlined the crime, appointed Henry Kramer and James Sprenger Inquisitors for Germany, and directed them to proceed with

[2] Translated by the Reverend Montague Summers and published by John Rodker in England (1928) in a limited edition of 1275 copies. I am indebted to Columbia University for the use of their copy. The book also contains a translation of the bull of Pope Innocent VIII, *Summis desiderantes affectibus* (1484), and a historical introduction by Father Summers. As amazing as the document itself is the argument which this scholarly writer of the present epoch makes for the infallibility of the papal bull and the justification of the campaign, even the belief in sorcery and the use of torture and fire, with some slight indication of revulsion at the savagery of the time and the inability to recognize insanity, on the ground that witchcraft constituted, along with heresy in general, a threat against civilization itself, comparable to Bolshevism in our time. Father Summers is also the author of a *Popular History of Witchcraft* (New York: E. P. Dutton & Co., 1937) and *The Geography of Witchcraft* (New York: Alfred A. Knopf, Inc., 1927).

vigor. Sporadic witchcraft had appeared in the Inquisition since the thirteenth century, but now it was identified with heresy and became a specific campaign. Kramer and Sprenger prepared the *Malleus Maleficarum* as an official guide. Issued in many editions, it influenced all subsequent books on magic and for two centuries determined the legal procedure against sorcery and witches.

The first part of the document argues at length the existence of devils and the power of witches, against the skepticism of certain physicians and clerics who were obstructing the Inquisition. So it is evident that a wiser counsel was available. Perhaps it is idle to speculate on the possibility, at that date in history, of a genuine program for popular education and the freedom of science. It was a time when scientists themselves were suspected of magic and persecuted for every deviation from Scholastic tradition. To doubt the existence of Satan and the truth of popular superstitions almost attained the status of heresy. It was thought to be a device of Satan and ground for grave suspicion. Part two of the *Malleus Maleficarum* reviews in great detail the works of witchcraft and the remedies prescribed by the Church for those who are bewitched. The last part of the treatise outlines the procedure of an examination—it must not be identified with a trial as that word is used among us today—and the forms of condemnation for culprits.

How many thousands of people were poisoned by witches brew and how many unbaptized babies were sacrificed in diabolic rites can never be estimated, but it is certainly probable that the number is not so large as the scores of thousands who were tortured and burned at the stake, garroted, or hung, one of the blackest pages of human history. Prosecutors never seem to have been primarily bent on discovering these acts against humanity as such. Their objective was to discover what a culprit believed and how he interpreted his own acts or the accusations made against him. It was a war of ideologies. The whole procedure was designed, even to the point of promising mercy with lying intent, to wring a confession from the accused; and one who reads the account will find no mystery in the way modern police states and totalitarian regimes secure their mysterious confessions. "Judicial" procedure is the same; methods of torture are said to be nowadays more subtle.

As the campaign proceeded, the doctrine of Satan acquired the solidity of dogma. The examinations and confessions produced a remarkable uniformity in lurid tales of traffic with demons, the black mass, the witch's Sabbath; and one must raise the question at least as to whether this uniformity was projected by the Inquisitors themselves. The learned doctors found it necessary to formulate clearly the thing they were looking for. It would be difficult to decide whether their notions about the works of Satan were based on what their witnesses reported, or rather that what they tortured out of their victims was molded by what the Inquisitors were looking for; probably both! But what they were looking for was also determined partly by an appeal to ancient authorities and traditions and partly by deductions from their own dogmatic theology. Satan and his kingdom must be the exact opposite of Christ, and the vices of witchcraft would naturally be the abominations of the Church.

So here is the picture which emerges: The devils can appear in human form, not real body, but condensed air and vapors. Usually they are black or red, with horns and a tail and always with cloven feet. They can transport people to distant places, especially for night revels, engage in copulation with both men and women, though nearly always with women, and they can transmute themselves and people into animal forms. The favorite disguises were a dog, a goat, or a fiery dragon for Satan himself; but often they appeared as a cat, a horse, mice, or even vermin. All this is in the book: didn't Satan turn into a serpent in the Garden, and transport

Jesus in the wilderness? And the demons cohabited with the daughters of men in the days of Noah. Then there is the compact with the devil, whose origin comes not from the Bible but from that infinite abyss of folklore in northern Europe. By this means a sorcerer gets the help of Satan, with a little black magic, to do marvelous things: he conjures the ancients, like Helen of Troy, harms his enemies, raises a hailstorm, or makes a cow go dry. By a devious logic it is even proved that children can be born from union with the devil, and they can be dedicated to Satan by midwives before baptism; hence numerous children went to the flames with their elders.

The sixteenth century produced the legendary Dr. Faustus and his pact with Mephistopheles, a name for Satan whose origin is unknown. Faustus lived in Germany as a contemporary of Luther and Melanchthon, frequenting the university towns and acquiring a reputation among the students for boasting and magic. The story of his life, as it finally passed into literature, acquired all the elements and fictional accretions of the age-old *Myth of the Magus*. This is shown by E. M. Butler in a book by that name, and he also traces the manner in which Christian thought influenced the evolution of the myth. The ancient magician was the hero and great leader, Zarathustra, Moses, Solomon, and the Magi; but Faust is the lowest of the low, vile enemy of everything held by the Church to be good.[3]

Bringing of the devil out of the shadows and endowing him with a definable personality and program was the final

[3] E. M. Butler of Cambridge University has made a valuable clarification of the complicated literature of magic ritual and mythology in *The Myth of the Magus* (New York: The Macmillan Co., 1948) and *Ritual Magic* (London: Cambridge University Press, 1949). Both volumes give a critical review of the Faust legend and the magical ritual which developed in the Faustian period. The former volume (pp. 136 ff.) reviews the relations between Catholic and Protestant influences on demonolatry in the sixteenth century. The last chapter of the latter volume is a review of the myth of Satanism with respect to the modern conflicts between the churches and the secret orders.

step in the modern rejection of the myth of Satanism. The last witch was executed in England in 1682, and the same year Louis XIV put an end to capital punishment for sorcery in France. But mythology has a thousand lives in folklore. Sporadic witch hunts and executions continued into the eighteenth century in Europe. Persecutions and murders in Europe and America are still occasionally traceable to belief in Satan and the practice of black magic. In the eighteenth century a considerable literature of satire on the devil appeared. A *Dialogue of Devils* published anonymously in London in 1751 indicated that devils have a remarkable insight into British politics and personalities of the theater. Daniel Defoe is credited with *The History of the Devil* (1793) which spiritualizes Satan and finds his chief sphere of activity in politics. Defoe pours contempt on folk tales and dramatic portrayals of devils, calling them "chimney-corner divinity."

The Catholic Church shifted its campaign against Satan from the wizards and witches to the secret societies which came into prominence during the Age of Enlightenment. Secret rituals, it is said, can be traced to patterns of ancient magic, which, if one goes back far enough, are often confused with religion. To this day secret orders are often maligned as the synagogue of Satan.

Milton's Satan

David Masson develops an instructive contrast between the devils of Luther, Milton, and Goethe, spanning a little more than three centuries of literary history. Luther's devil was experimental, scriptural, and actually existing, the common devil of sixteenth-century educated men. Milton's Satan is an epic hero. Milton's poems are the most complete literary statement of the Satan myth, though it is not quite certain whether he regarded the belief as mythical. In Goethe, the "scheming, enthusiastic archangel has been soured and civilized into the clever coldhearted Mephistopheles"; he is "the spirit of evil in modern society," the cosmic Satan become a personal devil, and he is a purely dramatic character.[4]

Paradise Lost gives us a portrait of the Evil One which for grandeur and pathos, dignity and degradation, is not equaled by any other hero in literature. Milton's Satan is the orthodox devil at his best, stripped of all fantastic caricatures which belong to popular fancy, and drawn in terms of self-conscious evil, pride, jealousy, and the will to rebellion, combined with tragic despair; the personification of what one might call the higher or at least the more refined forms of evil, not that they are on that account any less evil. He is not the gross and malicious devil; he is the studious and reflective psychological devil. In the care with which he details his "magnificent rebel," Milton reflects something of the struggle in his own breast, and in his own society, against the absolutistic pretensions of the Stuart dynasty in England.

With all the Puritan's devotion to Scripture, it is remarkable that Milton did not seem to realize how much he was embellishing the Biblical text, and modern readers have often been misled into thinking that his hero is the Biblical Satan. But Milton faithfully presents the orthodox Christian position on the nature and origin of evil. Paradise is lost, both for Satan and for man, by the rebellion of the will, by its weakness in resisting the inner temptations of pride, vanity, and self-interest. The scene is laid in heaven and in the Garden of Eden. The possibility of Paradise Regained is awakened by the coming of one among men whom all the subtle arts of Satan cannot reduce to servitude. The scene for that is the encounter of Christ with the devil in the wilderness. Milton's epic power reaches its height in the first poem, but from the point of view of modern religion the second deserves a larger measure of consideration. It is a mas-

[4] David Masson, The Three Devils (London: Macmillan & Co., 1874), p. 39.

terful portrayal of the subjective struggle of man with evil. For many moderns, the evolutionary philosophy has set aside the standpoint of a Paradise lost. One cannot lose what he has never had; but he might gain it; and if Paradise is ever to be gained, man must take the path of moral struggle toward the victory achieved by Jesus in the wilderness.

Mephistopheles

Modernists find a more compatible conception in Goethe's *Faust*. Mephistopheles is no fallen Lucifer nor brimstone-scented Satan. He is the modern cultured devil as he says himself, in the Witches' Kitchen scene:

> Culture, which smooth the whole world licks,
> Also unto the Devil sticks.
> The days of that old Northern phantom now are over:
> Where canst thou horns and tail and claws discover? [5]

Mephistopheles is fond of philosophizing, and thus his nature is elaborated. Goethe paid tribute to Milton's conception, but rejected it. Mephistopheles is neither the proud rebel against an intolerable divine autocracy nor the jealous seducer of man, whose high position in the cosmos threatens his own self-conceit. Rather, he is the fully painted figure of the cynical Satan of the Book of Job. Goethe goes back to the provisional dualism of ancient Israel. His devil is no irreconcilable enemy of God, tossed out of heaven. He is

> Part of that Power, not understood,
> Which always wills the Bad, and always works the Good.

A Prologue in Heaven opens the drama, like the Book of Job, where a wager over the soul of Faust is laid, and then the Lord acknowledges a creative function for Satan, revealing also Goethe's theory of the highest good for man:

[5] All quotations are from Bayard Taylor's translation of *Faust* in the Modern Library Edition (New York: Random House, Inc., 1948).

Of all the bold, denying Spirits,
The waggish knave least trouble doth create.
Man's active nature, flagging, seeks too soon the level;
Unqualified repose he learns to crave;
Whence, willingly, the comrade him I gave,
Who works, excites, and must create, as Devil.

The speeches of Mephisto are all replete with Goethe's acute diagnosis of the ills which afflict human existence, and the very cynical analysis is at least an intellectual contribution toward their alleviation.

McKechnie in the work previously quoted (Chapter 3), points out a sharp difference between Goethe's devil and Job's Satan. Mephistopheles is the fair-weather devil, one who tempts men in times of prosperity. He "is an angler for the souls of men, and the malicious patience of his angling is more to be dreaded than the frightfulness of Satan." Job had to survive such a tempter, but then had to suffer from the rain of evil out of heaven and nature. For Goethe, the modernist and the romanticist, not nature but man's mismangement of life is the source of evil; and whatever salvation is available to him must be won by struggle in the moral and social sphere through which Faust is drawn by Mephisto.

Faust is an old professor who has fallen into an academic despair which every professor understands, and he seeks by magic to salvage some meaning from life. When Mephistopheles appears, he turns out to be the philosophical pessimist:

I am the Spirit that Denies!
And justly so: for all things, from the Void
Called forth, deserve to be destroyed:
'T were better, then, were naught created.

F. C. S. Schiller, the Oxford pragmatist, in his *Humanism* wrote an essay on Mephistopheles in which he says that his pessimism is profound because it is complete intellectualism —source of all deviltry for the pragmatist—and it is cheerful because it is an ancient and sophisticated pessimism. He is not seriously interested in winning Faust for the infernal regions, the defeat of which is forecast in the Prologue. He is out simply to demonstrate the inaneness of existence and to have a good time doing it. His fundamental axiom is the seductive statement of the serpent to Eve, written in Latin into the student's notebook when he impersonates the professor (not the serpent this time):

> Eritis sicut Deus, scientes bonum et malum.
> (Ye shall be as God, knowing good and evil).

Mephisto, then, becomes by indirection, if not by deliberate intention, the instrument of Faust's redemption by injecting into the jaded professor that *Streben*, key word for Goethe's philosophy, which carries him out of the halls of contemplation into the world of action. Faust pursues the common aims of men on four levels, under the guidance of this devil and with the aid of magical arts: first, sensuality and lust, then wealth and power, and then the pursuit of classic art forms in which Helen of Greece is brought forth from Hades and Faust falls in love with her (as Goethe was in love with classic art). Finally, Faust joins the great modern pursuit of social redemption, seeking a society provided with plenty and living in happiness on land wrested from the sea by engineering genius. Even this is fraught with tragedy, a peculiarly modern type of tragedy, yet also ancient, for it happened also at Naboth's Vineyard. A pious old couple with a cottage and chapel by the sea obstruct the dream of Utopia, and fall in the flames of "progress"!

Blissful contemplation of the humanitarian dream, however, produces the final climax when Faust cries to the fleeting moment, "Ah, still delay—thou art so fair!" and the wager is lost, the bond to Satan is forfeited, and Faust falls down dead. Even as he lingers over the body before trying to snatch the soul, Mephisto philosophizes on the nihilism of time and the emptiness of life:

Past and pure Naught, complete monotony!
What good for us, this endlessly creating?—
What is created then annihilating?
"And now it's past!" Why read a page so twisted?
'T is just the same as if it ne'er existed,
Yet goes in circles round as if it had, however:
I'd rather choose, instead, the Void forever.

The intervention of heavenly hosts cheats the devil of his due, and he and his minions, swarming out of the mouth of hell around Faust, are driven back into the pit by a shower of roses, and the soul of Faust is carried into the heavens with angel songs of salvation:

The noble Spirit now is free,
And saved from evil scheming:
Whoe'er aspires unweariedly
Is not beyond redeeming.
And if he feels the grace of Love
That from on high is given,
The Blessed Hosts, that wait above,
Shall welcome him to heaven.

Thus salvation is not because of merit, but the pure grace of God; not even the merit of the humanitarian dream, though that alone can produce the moment of pure human bliss. Goethe shows his loyalty to the central Christian tradition, with this exception: he never brings Faust to any act or attitude of repentance. This omission indicates one of the main defects of romantic and humanistic religion.

Critics have subjected Goethe's devotion to nature, and his notion of salvation by striving, to searching analysis. The selfish egotism and individualism of Faust's *Streben* are a glaring weakness to all prophets of the social gospel.[6] Many seem to hold that no miracle would be necessary for salvation if man would fully devote himself to humanitarianism; merit

[6] For one of the best of these see R. T. Flewelling, *Christ and the Dramas of Doubt* (New York: Abingdon-Cokesbury Press, 1913), Chap. xii-xv.

might mitigate to some extent the pure necessity of grace. But events of the twentieth century have shown the Naboth's Vineyard episode to be a very minor portrayal of what man is capable of in the name of humanity and democracy. For the promise of Utopia, whole populations have been displaced and minority groups liquidated by the millions. Goethe, in spite of his own devotion to aestheticism and humanity as a sort of personal religion, at least got a glimpse of the complicated and ambiguous situation of man as he faces the problem of human activity.

The Devil for Modernists

Mephistopheles has few flaws from the modern point of view, however; he is a superb embodiment of the moral struggle as it has existed in the liberal industrial culture, an age which now may have come to an end. The humanistic spirit led religious thought back to provisional dualism. Brimstone hell passed out of theology, hell-fire out of the pulpits, and the imprecatory Psalms are no more in the pews. F. C. S. Schiller, reviving an ancient suggestion of the Greek Church Father Origen, even went so far as to suggest that attention be given to the salvation of Satan. It is said that Goethe entertained the proposal, but thought his contemporaries would not tolerate the notion.

Perhaps this is but to say that when religion becomes philosophical it really has little use for the idea of Satan. A. C. Knudson, in his The Doctrine of Redemption,[7] states the matter for the rational tradition when he says,

> Satan occupies no logical place in the Christian system of belief. His existence does not explain the origin of sin nor does it make temptation any more intelligible. In so far as it implies a nonhuman source of human sin, it is a relic of dualism and cancels the concept of sin.

[7] (New York: Abingdon-Cokesbury Press, 1933), p. 251. Quoted by permission.

But rational criticism does not yet seem adequate to exorcise the demons. They grow out of human soil where the spade of reason is not adequate to reach the roots. Across the world, in the Orient, in the islands, in the southland, men build their houses and erect their temples in a manner to ward off the malevolence of evil spirits. Even in "enlightened" America, the worshippers of Satan have been known to break into Christian churches to hold their modernized version of Walpurgis Night. An American novelist like Theodore Dreiser, devotee of naturalism though he was, when he came up against the naked depravity of the human spirit had recourse to the Christian devil. In *An American Tragedy*, he presented the tragic moral conflicts of our society in a poignant episode. At the moment when Clyde Griffith is first struck by the thought of murdering his sweetheart as a means of release from his predicament, Dreiser introduced a parenthesis, "(what devil's whisper?—what evil hint of an evil spirit?)." The idea of Satan will continue to stand for the dark and demonic aspects of human experience. "The devil's cleverest wile is to convince us that he does not exist," said Baudelaire, and Denis de Rougemont thinks this is the "most profound observation on Satan written by a modern." [8] The Frenchman has recently written *The Devil's Share*, a clever statement of the demonic aspects of our world and an argument that liberal interpretations are inadequate because belief in the reality of Satan has been given up. He is joined by two Englishmen who have published books in America which brilliantly expound the reality of devils and their works: William Robinson, *The Devil and God*,[9] would reinstate the Biblical point of view; C. S. Lewis brought the devils to life in *The Screwtape Letters*, and in *The Problem*

[8] Denis de Rougemont, *The Devil's Share* (New York: Pantheon Books, Inc., 1944).
[9] (New York: Abingdon-Cokesbury Press, 1945).

of *Pain* he states his belief in their reality.[10] Satan is not quite so manifest to Americans as to Europeans at the present time, it would seem, but one at least has joined them. Edwin Lewis in *The Creator and the Adversary* comes to the conclusion that there is a "tragic dilemma of the divine. God cannot act creatively without making it possible for the demonic to act discreatively." [11]

Two European novelists who enjoy great popularity among Americans have written vivid portraits of the devil. Dostoevski's devil is a shopworn member of the Russian gentry who appears in a phantom to Ivan Karamazov, plaguing him with all his own rejected philosophic nihilism.[12] Thomas Mann, in his *Dr. Faustus*, has written of the devil as though he were as real as God:

> ... Wherever theology is, ... there too the devil belongs to the picture and asserts his complementary reality to that of God. It is easy to say that a modern theologian takes him "symbolically." In my view theology cannot be modern—one may reckon that to its advantage, of course—and as for symbolism, I cannot see why one should take hell more symbolically than heaven. The people have certainly never done so. Always the crass, obscenely comic figure of the "divel" has been nearer to them than the Eternal Majesty. . . .[13]

Mann's devil has red hair and speaks only in old German out of respect for a country which has always had a special respect for him.

If our account of the psychological origin of the idea of Satan is correct (Chapter 4, p. 66), then we shall expect to find devils at every stage of human culture, for the struggle

10 (New York: The Macmillan Co., 1943 and 1944).

11 (New York: Abingdon-Cokesbury Press, 1948), p. 138.

12 *The Brothers Karamazov* (New York: Random House, Inc., 1948), Book XI, Chap. ix.

13 Thomas Mann, *Doctor Faustus* (New York: Alfred A. Knopf, Inc., 1948), p. 96. This is, of course, the sentiment which Mann attributes to the narrator of the story. Although this cannot be asserted as the conviction of the author, nevertheless it precisely states the point of view of that profound narrative.

of the inner life is always the same; only the symbols change. Carl Sandburg represents the contemporary poetic treatment of evil in his "Wilderness." His devils are the hairy and scaly-faced ghosts of our biological ancestry:

> There is a wolf in me . . . fangs pointed for tearing gashes . . . a red tongue for raw meat . . . and the hot lapping of blood—I keep this wolf because the wilderness gave it to me and the wilderness will not let it go.

> There is a fox in me . . . a silver-gray fox . . . I sniff and guess . . . I pick things out of the wind and air . . . I nose in the dark night and take sleepers and eat them and hide the feathers . . . I circle and loop and double-cross.

> There is a hog in me . . . a snout and a belly . . . a machinery for eating and grunting . . . a machinery for sleeping satisfied in the sun—I got this too from the wilderness and the wilder-- ness will not let it go.

> There is a fish in me . . . I know I came from salt-blue water gates . . . I scurried with shoals of herring . . . I blew water- spouts with porpoises . . . before land was . . . before Noah . . . before the first chapter of Genesis.

> There is a baboon in me . . . clambering-clawed . . . dog-faced . . . yawping a galoot's hunger . . . hairy under the armpits . . . here are the hawk-eyed hankering men . . . here are the blond and blue-eyed women . . . here they hide curled asleep waiting . . . ready to snarl and kill . . . ready to sing and give milk . . . waiting—I keep the baboon because the wilderness says so.

> There is an eagle in me and a mockingbird . . . and the eagle flies among the Rocky Mountains of my dreams and fights among the Sierra crags of what I want . . . and the mocking- bird warbles in the early forenoon before the dew is gone, warbles in the underbrush of my Chattanoogas of hope, gushes over the blue Ozark foothills of my wishes—And I got the eagle and the mockingbird from the wilderness.

> O, I got a zoo, I got a menagerie, inside my ribs, under my bony head, under my red-valve heart—and I got something else: it is a man-child heart, a woman-child heart: it is a father and mother and lover: it came from God-Knows-

Where: it is going to God-Knows-Where—For I am the
keeper of the zoo: I say yes and no: I sing and kill and work:
I am a pal of the world: I came from the wilderness.[14]

Though names and faces change, the problem remains
the same: the fox, the hog, the baboon, or the inferiority
complex has to be exorcised and subdued no less than the
fiery dragon or horned diablerie; and sometimes modern
procedures, whether in psychiatrist's parlor or monk's cell,
are in no essential different from ancient incantation and
amulet.

[14] Sandburg's "Wilderness" is in the volume called *Cornhuskers* (New
York: Henry Holt & Co., 1918).

Chapter 6

EVIL AND THE PARADOX OF RELIGION

The uncertain and equivocal position of man in his wordly existence has never been more profoundly stated than in the Book of Job:

> Truly I know that it is so:
>   But how can a man be just before God?
> If one wished to contend with him,
>   one could not answer him once in a thousand times.
>
>   *   *   *   *   *
>
> If I wash myself with snow,
>   and cleanse my hands with lye,
> yet thou wilt plunge me into a pit,
>   and my own clothes will abhor me. (9:2-3, 30-31)

The human being is firmly planted in the clay. As an organism, he struggles into life out of the muck—and the emphasis must be put on *struggle*. If his struggles are vigorous enough, soon he comes to consciousness and to freedom. He reaches for the moon and then for the stars, and knowing good and evil, he feels himself akin to the gods; then he falls into sin by aspiring to be one.

> Thy hands fashioned and made me;
>   and now thou dost turn about and destroy me.
> Remember that thou hast made me of clay;
>   and wilt thou turn me to dust again?
> Didst thou not pour me out like milk
>   and curdle me like cheese?
> Thou didst clothe me with skin and flesh,
>   and knit me together with bones and sinews.
> Thou hast granted me life and steadfast love;
>   and thy care has preserved my spirit.

> Yet these things thou didst hide in thy heart;
>   I know that this was thy purpose.
> If I sin, thou dost mark me,
>   and dost not acquit me of my iniquity.
> If I am wicked, woe to me!
>   If I am righteous, I cannot lift up my head,
> for I am filled with disgrace
>   and look upon my affliction.
> And if I lift myself up, thou dost hunt me like a lion
>   and again work wonders against me; (10:8-16)

Man never shakes off the clay and the muck from his feet; he is bound to biological nature, but his spirit is in the clouds.

Yet there is another side to the story: God reaches for man. And this, too, is in the Book of Job, though not in the words of Job. He is caught in the whirling torrent, and cries out for an understanding deity whom he does not quite apprehend. Neither is it to be found in the didactic moralism of the friends. They are also enmeshed in the mess of things. Eliphaz comes near to the word of comfort in his first speech, but from there the dispute over justice waxes bitter and holds their attention. After Job subsides in despair, God answers from the whirlwind in a way which will occupy our attention later; but this reach of God for man is also set forth by Elihu, the youth of the drama who is much neglected by commentators, in a passage of beauty to match anything in the book:

> If there be for him an angel,
>   a mediator, one of the thousand,
>   to declare to man what is right for him;
> and he is gracious to him, and says,
>   "Deliver him from going down into the Pit,
>   I have found a ransom;
> let his flesh become fresh with youth;
>   let him return to the days of his youthful vigor."
> Then man prays to God, and he accepts him,
>   he comes into his presence with joy. (33:23-26)

The Dilemma of Evil

Here is a paradox which solves a paradox (if that may be allowed in logic); for not only is the position of man in existence paradoxical, but the grace of God is a paradox. But to put the matter more clearly and accurately, we have here the paradox with which the Christian confronts the dilemma of evil. That dilemma was probably presented first to the Western world, and most sharply, in the materialistic and atheistic poem of Lucretius, *De Rerum Natura*, discussed in Chapter 3. David Hume, in his famous *Dialogues Concerning Natural Religion*, formulated the argument of Lucretius into a logical dilemma:

> Epicurus' old questions are yet unanswered.
> Is he [God] willing to prevent evil, but not able? then is he impotent. Is he able, but not willing? then is he malevolent. Is he both able and willing? whence then is evil.

One way to counter a dilemma is to affirm a paradox in which you take the alternatives of the dilemma by both horns, and that is precisely what the religious faith of Christianity has traditionally done for this skeptic's dilemma. It has confidently affirmed that God is both able and willing, omnipotent and benevolent, but it is a paradox and the meaning of evil is shrouded in mystery.

A dilemma is a predicament in which one must choose between two or more propositions, either of which entails results contrary to reason or desire. A paradox is the affirmation of two propositions which are not in complete logical agreement with each other. One may escape from a dilemma in other ways than by grabbing both horns, notably by finding an alternative outlet between the horns. Some may say that Christian theology has done this by introducing the element of time into the unfolding of God's purposes: what seems now to be evil and a complete frustration of all good design will turn out in the future to be good, a future, of course, which is hidden in divine mystery. But it is just this mystery which renders the proposition of God's power and goodness a paradox from a point of view within strict reasoning.

The use of the word paradox as applied to such theological matters is modern. It comes about from the narrowing of the definition of reason to exclude faith. Reason in current usage comprehends what we know, not what we must believe purely on faith. It has not always been so, and it is not so universally today. Such paradoxical propositions were mysteries and dogmas in Scholastic theology, not contrary to reason but beyond it. In that case, reason is what Professor L. Harold DeWolf defines as "unlimited comprehensive coherence," to which concepts of faith are admitted on the basis of their freedom from contradiction and their contribution to the whole synoptic view.[1] If reason can assimilate the dogmas of faith, or if faith can overcome the skepticism of reason, so that the two live together in peace, some would hold that the paradoxes have been resolved.

There would seem to be two gains, however, from the current recognition that religious thought rests to some extent on paradoxes: one is that it has a tendency to pull ancient religious concepts out from behind the veil of dogma and mystery for critical examination. A paradox is not a place where the rational mind can rest. It is a perpetual challenge. We affirm it and then we deny it. We take first this horn and then the other, and end our criticism by clinging to both, in much the same way that St. Augustine clung both to free will and then to determinism as he faced the

[1] L. Harold DeWolf, *The Religious Revolt Against Reason* (New York: Harper & Bros., 1949), pp. 197 ff. This work is an incisive criticism of the existential theologies which emphasize the paradoxical basis of religious faith, but the last chapter on "Reason and Faith" will not be accepted by all as a solution of the question.

critics of each. And a second gain is that contemporary literature, which does not balk at a paradox, in the same manner as the Book of Job, would seem to be a little more realistic in facing the enigmatic situation in which man is placed in existence. The easy wedding of faith and reason has always had a tendency to lull man to sleep in the seductive arms of spiritual pride.

The Paradox in Job

No writer in modern times has more firmly grasped the paradoxical situation than Dostoevski, and he must have got hold of it to some extent from the Book of Job. In *The Brothers Karamazov*, the dying monk, when commending the Bible to his brethren, centers their interest on the Book of Job:

> Good heavens, what a book it is, and what lessons there are in it! . . . I've never been able to read that sacred tale without tears. And how much that is great, mysterious and unfathomable there is in it! . . . The greatness of it lies just in the fact that it is a mystery—that the passing earthly show and the eternal verity are brought together in it. In the face of the earthly truth, the eternal truth is accomplished.[2]

What is this paradox as it confronts us in the Book of Job? It is not the theological formulation of God's power and goodness; that comes at the climax of religious history. Job's God is the Almighty, whose wisdom and goodness are open to question and shrouded in inscrutable mystery. We must formulate the paradox of Job on the level of human experience.

What is happening on the ash heap? The pitiful struggle of man in the midst of his uncertain existence is analyzed, not by philosophers sitting in the plush and velvet of a

[2] From Garnett's translation in the Modern Student's Library (New York: Random House, Inc.), p. 347 f.

Rembrandt philosophers' sanctum but by poets who sit on the ash heap itself. Even when Job is fenced about with all the protections of providence, life is still a struggle to win a living out of the wilderness, to rear a family, to build the good community, fraught not only with hostile external enemies, but with temptations to sin and to renounce God secretly, which must be propitiated with much trembling and sacrifice. And all these values are then destroyed in one satanic blast. Job and his friends try to penetrate the veil of understanding. The venom and bitterness of the skeptic heart are poured out in poetic dirge, and beams of insight illumine the mind, yet reason never achieves a theodicy.

This is the first horn of the paradox: the struggle for the good life here on the earth is inspired and sustained by a religious impulse, the reach of man away from the clod toward God.

Then God reaches out for Job. The groping of man and the reach of God do not always make connection. That is obvious to these poets, and to them the groping of man is the more poignant. We do not have here a great classical statement of the reach of God for man, as in the fifty-third chapter of Isaiah or the passion story of St. Matthew's gospel. But Job's extremity is God's opportunity, and the poets rise to the highest level of numinous feeling when they present the voice from the whirlwind. The spiritual tempest is stilled; faith is restored as a tiny spark: "Now my eye sees thee!" And when God confronts man, it is always in judgment: I "repent in dust and ashes."

This is the second horn of the paradox. At the moment of collapse and crisis, religious faith presents man with "the vision of God which makes further dialectic unnecessary." [3]

[3] A phrase given to me in a personal conversation about Job with Dr. Lynn Harold Hough. In the second chapter we have paid our respects to those interpreters of the Book of Job who find all the values in the skeptical debate with the friends and regard the theophany as producing only an impotent collapse in Job.

Man Reaching for God

We must go over this paradox more carefully and elaborate it more fully. In its initial phase, religion must be described as a vision of the good life and a struggle for its realization. Like the Brothers Karamazov, we can accept God simply but we cannot accept his world. We strive to win a living and build a home in some wilderness; we strive for moral integrity and personal holiness in an existence which is always problematic and uncertain; we long for the ideal community in an immoral society; we labor to understand our universe through the researches of science and philosophy, all because we have a vision of the good life and we want to realize it for ourselves and for those depending upon us. The moral law, the prophetic vision, the tools of science, and the wisdom of philosophy become patterns for our idealism, the dream of a better world. Then we rear our altars and lift our hands in worship to those gods which embody our vision of the good, and in this way religion becomes a channel for a more-than-human inspiration to the struggle.

Religious institutions and the great seers have not all agreed upon the vision of the good, but among the greatest of them, Confucius, Buddha, Plato, Aristotle, Moses, the Hebrew prophets, and St. Paul, there has been some agreement, perhaps quite remarkable agreement, on intrinsic values, and each of them has contributed something important to our techniques of struggle for their realization.

In so far as religion is humanistic or prophetic, to use two words which have clear connotations in our tradition, it lays hold of this first horn of the paradox. Prophetic religion addresses itself to the moral problems of any time. Every man in the Western world who takes the name of a righteous God as inspiration for moral and social improvement treads the path set by those heroes of old who laid it upon the

hearts of the Hebrew race that Yahweh cares more for justice
and mercy than for smoking sacrifices.

> Bring no more vain offerings;
>   incense is an abomination to me.
> New moon and sabbath and the calling of assemblies—
>   I cannot endure iniquity and solemn assembly.
> Your new moons and your appointed feasts
>   my soul hates;
> they have become a burden to me,
>   I am weary of bearing them.
> When you spread forth your hands,
>   I will hide my eyes from you;
> even though you make many prayers,
>   I will not listen;
>   your hands are full of blood.
> Wash yourselves; make yourselves clean;
>   remove the evil of your doings;
>   from before my eyes;
> cease to do evil,
>   learn to do good;
> seek justice,
>   correct oppression;
> defend the fatherless,
>   plead for the widow. (Isaiah 1:13-17)

In a time like today, the Christian faith confronts us with
a vision of God in Christ calling us to make this world, its
moral and social life, its philosophies and aesthetic cultures,
his everlasting kingdom. For some interpreters of religion,
this is the realm of ethics as distinct from religion, touched
up a little by the theological reference. Some also would
stop here and say this is the whole of religion, so far as it can
have any significance for our time. Both are wrong. As soon
as man became "a face turned from the clod" he was religious, for there is no sharp distinction between ethics and
religion except as sophisticated man makes it by abstraction.
Man's primal vision of the good life is the face turned

toward God. One of the main things to remember about the Christian faith is that it covers life—it cannot be confined to a special realm of the religious, nor can ethical, aesthetic, or rational culture be excluded from it.

This is the first horn of the paradox, the human struggle for the good life. A second horn is equally essential.

God Reaching for Man

The key word in our first proposition is *struggle*. It never ceases. The pull is always upstream. At just the moment we think we have won the good life and lean on the oars for a rest, we begin to drift. No one ever reaches the goal. It is as though the ideal recedes from the advancing ship. In reality the ideal changes and its new form is always set farther than the reach.

But there is a deeper and darker aspect of the human situation than this elusiveness of the ideal. It was not the failure to reach an ideal which bedeviled Job. It was the ever-present impending dread of the demonic which led him to make continual sacrifices and prayers for the safety of his family. There is impending shipwreck, or to change the figure of speech, there are times when the whole wordly project of our dreams comes tumbling down around our ears in total wreck. That is our problem of evil. It is moral only in part, although a very significant part, as we shall see later, for one who attains moral self-confidence wins more than half the battle. Man seems to be caught in the crushing grasp of vast forces, both within and without, which bring him to what the prophets called "doom" and what modern theologians call "crisis."

There is not much sense in coming to Job on his ash heap and saying, "The trouble with you is that you did not struggle hard enough nor cleverly enough." An Eliphaz can always pick flaws even in the character or program of a perfect and upright man. But that does not quite answer the problem. War and pestilence and traffic accidents and a thousand demonic forces constantly keep the best of men trembling on the verge of that deep, dark chasm into which all worldly dreams are finally plunged.

Crisis is a better word than doom for the actual situation of man because of its timelessness. It is not a far-off final event; it is the impending failure or realization of its inevitability which may happen at any moment, and it comes many times both to individuals and to nations. It would not be correct to say that religion is simply preparation for crisis— it is the inspiration of life as well—but all true religion provides a means for transcending the crisis; what has always been known as the way of salvation. Just when all our struggles fail and all our petty schemes crash in ruin, the reach of God for man becomes more evident to him, or so it is under the revelation of a great religious faith. It is not quite correct, either, to call it a way of escape, for man never escapes the tragic situation even though he may escape some of the final punishments for his sinful involvement which an abstract justice would prescribe.

The ultimate issues of life are not settled by the report of the profit ledger, nor by the size of possessions, nor by the number and affluence of our children, nor even by the peace and prosperity of the nation and the world. Only the soul which has found peace in God, the conscience void of offense through grace, has come to the ultimate value of existence. And the key word in the second horn of our paradox is grace, for grace is the reach of God toward man.

The same Old Testament book which has been quoted above for its incisive statement of the moral struggle also includes these lofty words for the soul or the nation which has met its crisis:

Surely he has borne our griefs
 and carried our sorrows;
yet we esteemed him stricken,
 smitten by God, and afflicted.
But he was wounded for our transgressions,
 he was bruised for our iniquities;
upon him was the chastisement that made us whole,
 and with his stripes we are healed.
All we like sheep have gone astray;
 we have turned every one to his own way;
and the LORD has laid on him
 the iniquity of us all. (Isaiah 53:4-6)

The Apocalypse

The Holy Scriptures are full of such contrasts which represent the two horns of the paradox. But for fuller illustration of the second, let us turn to those passages which are known as apocalypticism. The Book of Daniel and the Revelation of Saint John are the two apocalyptic books, while many snatches of the same literary form and content are found in other books. Though these writings are much loved because of their power to speak to souls caught in the dark night of human despair, they are often misunderstood and frequently rejected as the authoritative Word of God.

The apocalyptic message is a philosophy of history which stands in sharp contrast to the social and ethical message of prophetism and to the predominant rationalism of the modern world view. The apocalyptist arises in the hour of crisis. Civilization is not just in decline; the breakdown has come. Everything is hopeless in history; but beyond the despair of the present order he sees a hidden revelation of ultimate destiny. God's in his heaven. All's not well with the world, but in his own time and in his own way God will take care of the faithful and blot out the wickedness of the world.

When Domitian, the mad Roman emperor, began his systematic campaign of extermination against the Christians in

95 A.D., everything looked absolutely black and hopeless for the faithful. Then the Apocalypse of Saint John was written to encourage the churches. It is an exhortation to steadfastness, no matter what the price of blood might be. The visions of the Seer on Patmos penetrate the veil which hides the face of destiny. The beast will be conquered and cast into the lake of brimstone; the New Jerusalem, taking the place of the Holy City so recently destroyed by Roman armies, will be let down from God out of heaven. Jasper walls and fountains of living water and no more tears will compensate the price of blood and iron.

Whatever our interpretation of these visions may be, whether we take them literally, allegorically, or historically, we have here an essential element in any true religion. Jeremiah faces the hostility of his countrymen, firm in preaching his message of doom; Socrates drinks the hemlock and comforts his friends in the Athenian jail; Jesus prays through the sweat of blood in Gethsemane; a thousand saints scorn the legions of Rome through the visions on Patmos; Saint Francis espouses Lady Poverty in a luxury-loving age; Martin Luther stands fearless before the Diet at Worms, though every tile on a housetop shelters a devil; Cranmer bathes his hands in the flames at Oxford; and the modern reformer defies the powers who would rob him of his living, all in the true confidence of religion that the failures of the faithful on earth will become the victories of heaven.

> Come, ye disconsolate, where'er ye languish;
> Come to the mercy seat, fervently kneel;
> Here bring your wounded hearts, here tell your anguish:
> Earth has no sorrow that Heaven cannot heal.

Christian history has been full of controversy over various systems of salvation. In our generation we have seen the effort to formulate the Christian religion without salvation. Our purpose now does not include a review of theories of salvation, such as the sacrificial, the sacerdotal, or the salvation by faith, but simply to say that without some doctrine of salvation in crisis we do not have the Christian faith.

Is It a Paradox?

The paradoxical nature of these two propositions still requires exposition: struggle for the good life, and salvation from the results of failure. There are ways of stating the second so that it does not seem so paradoxical. "God helps those who help themselves." "Salvation is in accordance with merit; if man is worthy of it, God will take care of him." That is the way Eliphaz and Bildad and Zophar put the matter. The ways of God are set by his character of exact justice. But this is purely theoretical; life does not turn out that way. The Christian faith promises Paradise to the penitent thief on the cross. There is no such thing as adequate merit. Man's salvation is impossible except for the reach of divine grace.

It would seem, then, that if we can count on escape from damnation, why should we struggle? Why not take things easier in the moral conflicts of life if divine favor is available through mystic rites or magic formulae? But that is putting the matter in an extreme form not justified by the teachings of religion. Salvation is not promised for rites or formulae, and these became magical only when they are employed to gain some personal advantage in the present. They are valuable for salvation only if they assist the spirit of man to apprehend the divine grace. But even if grace is available through faith alone, why should we pay the price of moral endeavor?

There seems to be no answer to that question but to affirm the paradox. Any religion which stops short of the double affirmation will be unsatisfactory to man's need for faith. In the religious fellowship we do not credit a profession, no matter how pious the testimony, where there is no lively interest in good works. "Not every one who says to me, 'LORD, LORD,' shall enter the kingdom of heaven, but he who does the will of my Father who is in heaven." We offer grace to the repentant sinner even on his deathbed, yet we demand as a religious obligation that man be good, always knowing that he will not be quite good enough.

The clashing crosscurrents of religious thought today are mainly due to overemphasis, sometimes the exclusive emphasis, on one or the other of these two phases of the religious paradox. Some forms of humanism repudiate theology and all supernaturalism and cling desperately to the first horn. They look upon dreams of supernal bliss as wishful thinking, and pin all hope for here or hereafter upon man, upon his innate capacities for moral and social idealism and his ability to master the methods of science for the solution of his problems. Max Otto would make a religion as well as a philosophy out of The Human Enterprise, title of one of his books, a religion without God and at enmity with all supernaturalism. So long as this program rides along on the residue of Christian love and charity in our culture, there is much to commend it. At the least, all men should do everything to cooperate in the effort to extend the fruits of scientific understanding to every phase of human enterprise.

A fatal defect in such humanism is the idolatry of men. They cherish their ideals as reals and invest their institutions with absoluteness. Even the emancipation from philosophical absolutism afforded by pragmatism can hardly suppress this proclivity. It is rooted in self-love, "the inclination of the human heart to solve the problem of the ambiguity of human existence by denying man's finiteness." This is the way Reinhold Niebuhr has put the matter, and a recurring theme in his preaching and writing has been the devastation wrought in history by putting institutions, both church and state, beyond criticism, the vehicle of ultimate reality and the promise of Utopia.[4] This has been Niebuhr's most important contri-

[4] The quotation is from Faith and History (New York: Chas. Scribner's Sons, 1949), p. 114. Chap. xii, "False Absolutes," is one of the best of Niebuhr's many statements of this social theory.

bution to social philosophy. Communism is a form of humanism which affords the most apparent and tragic illustration today. In the name of the classless and stateless Utopia, it has deified a military totalitarianism in which every weapon against freedom acquires moral sanction; the end justifies the means. It is by no means certain that democratic secularism in America has adequate safeguards against the same form of tyranny. The only principle of criticism is the conscious recognition at all times that man stands in an uncertain and paradoxical position of crisis and judgment.

On the other hand, all Christian orthodoxy and neosupernaturalism stand in danger of becoming mere escape mechanisms. When Karl Marx described religion as the opiate of the people, he put his finger unerringly upon the one-sidedness of nineteenth-century Christianity in Europe, to say nothing of much of it in the world today. It has cultivated a kind of transcendental hedonism which might be freely characterized by the line from the song once popularized by the International Workers of the World: "Ther'll be pie in the sky, by and by." The story of the way in which the Church has stood as a bulwark of defense, first for the institutions of feudal society and then for those of bourgeois society, is not a happy one. Christianity has never been leaven for the Promethean mass of the people in the Western world. It has followed too literally the prescription of St. Paul, "Therefore come out from them and be separate from them."

I once spent several days as a visitor in a Trappist monastery, the New Mellery Abbey near Dubuque, Iowa, and a pleasant interlude it was from the turmoil of the world, even the early hour for morning devotions from 2 to 5 A.M. The whole life of the brothers, as the host monk explained to me, is oriented to death. And why not? One is alive a very short time and he will be dead a very long time. But if this is wisdom at all, it is so for only a very small minority. Even the Trappist does not proclaim it as a program for all. And one comes away from the abbey with the feeling that a simpler faith might answer the problem of death if one were more rationally devoted to building the kingdom of God on earth.

There are other terms than paradox which might apply to this situation in religion. It has been called bipolarity. W. E. Hocking presents a principle of alternation in *The Meaning of God in Human Experience*.[5] I believe the theologian Ritschl is the source for the description of religion as an ellipse with two foci, not a circle with a single center, God at one focus and man at the other.[6] These symbols imply that there is a traceable circumference which defines and relates the poles or foci. If so, it must be apprehended by faith, not by reason. Therefore we stick to paradox as a better word to designate what actually confronts us when we try to interpret the situation of a man like Job and the function of religion in relation to it.

This does not commit us to irrationalism. Even Kierkegaard said that "the paradox is a source of the thinker's passion, and the thinker without a paradox is like a lover without feeling: a paltry mediocrity."[7] It was not a puny collapse of logic which led him and his followers to exhibit man in existence as caught in such paradoxes. Nor, on the other hand, does belief in reason mean that man cannot escape idolatry. Harold DeWolf, in his incisive examination of this problem, has put the matter very well:

> The vain and idolatrous pride of which rational believers are so often accused may at times be present, but reason has a cure for it. Will not reason teach man humility before his Maker? . . . Is it not the very purpose of reason to provide a continuing criticism of our own vain desires and unsupportable opinions?

[5] William E. Hocking, *The Meaning of God in Human Experience* (New Haven: Yale University Press, 1912), Chap. xxviii.

[6] I am indebted to Dr. A. C. Knudson for this. See his *The Principles of Christian Ethics* (New York: Abingdon-Cokesbury Press, 1943), p. 138.

[7] Sören A. Kierkegaard, *Philosophical Fragments* (Princeton: Princeton University Press, 1946), p. 29.

When we deny the validity of reason as instrument of religious knowledge, we then open the door wide to a species of vanity which holds itself immune to all criticism. Certainly pride is not unknown among religious irrationalists.[8]

In any case, we must lay firm hold upon both horns; reason being the chief instrument of the one and faith of the other. The glory of Job was his fearless rationalism when confronted by his comforters, but it took a very irrational whirlwind to confront him with God and bring him to humility. The necessity is like that of the cowboy in the game of bull-dogging. The intrepid sportsman of the western plains rides his horse along the side of a running Longhorn steer, plunges off the saddle onto the animal's neck, and grabbing the horns, rides it to the ground, holding it until it is tied. It is a dangerous and impossible feat unless the rider succeeds in catching and clinging doggedly to both horns.

Free Will and Determinism

The paradox involved in religion's attack upon the problem of evil may be recognized as a practical variation of the conflict which appears in philosophic history as the paradox of free will and determinism. Though this formulation is not to be found in the Book of Job, it is well to look at it in terms of more recent history.

Lewis White Beck, in the introduction to his translation of Kant's *Critique of Practical Reason*,[9] declares that our dependence on science today rests on a paradox which Kant saw more clearly than anyone else. Perhaps he would over-persuade us that one must go through Kant to the study of our problem, but he has set an important clue for understanding that modern sage.

[8] L. Harold DeWolf, *op. cit.*, pp. 115 ff.
[9] Immanuel Kant, *Critique of Practical Reason and Other Writings in Moral Philosophy*, translated and edited by Lewis White Beck (Chicago: University of Chicago Press, 1949).

What is this paradox on which scientific culture rests? The first horn is the nature of the objective world as it is understood through the methods of science. Its presupposition is that the world is a mechanism, operating in accordance with the principles of determinism. Mathematical logic is sufficient to interpret all problems of causality. First this was applied to physics, then extended to biology and finally to psychology, so that even human behavior is brought to some extent under the terms of mechanical interpretation and prediction. The mathematical conquest of reality is by no means complete, and in psychology on the one hand and astrophysics on the other it has been vastly complicated since the time of Newton and Kant, but fundamentally the principles of interpretation are not changed. Nature operates according to its own laws without the need of a transcendent ruler or supernatural purposes.

Then all this knowledge thus compiled is presented to man for his use—and this is the second horn of the paradox —in accordance with the inner and subjective conditions of knowledge and the purposes which belong to free consciousness. These are never out where they can be observed by the scientists, even those studying human behavior. As man anticipates the use he is going to make of his knowledge and the power it gives him, and as he introspects his self-conscious processes while doing it, he is aware of design and alternative choices. Then arises the questions of value and obligation. This is what has always been meant by freedom of the will.

There are two levels of this freedom. First, there is simply the manipulation of things in accordance with some specific design. Man has vast potentiality for this, but it is not essentially different from the freedom which biologists discover in the animal world, such as the wasp which used a pebble to batten down the mud door on its cocoon after repeated frustrations by the experimenter, or the ape that uses a stick

or a series of boxes to reach its food. Animal trainers capital-
ize on this freedom when they trot forth in the circus the
talking dog or the counting horse.

But freedom reaches a second and higher level for man
when he is presented with vast power of knowledge which
can be used for construction or destruction. He cannot ab-
solve himself from obligation by saying, "All energy is controlled by laws of its own nature, I have no responsibility."
He is confronted with the ultimate meaning and value of
existence itself. The Atomic Energy Commission, the military high command, and Congressional committees which
formulate the policies of government are not the only ones
who must become free at the level of critical judgment; all
citizens who participate in public opinion must accept the
obligation.

Man lives in two worlds, the world of things and the world
of free spirits. He is free and yet he is not free. And it is not
as though he were half free and half determined, nor any
other proportion, such as one to three. Every act, after it has
happened, can be interpreted retrospectively in accordance
with stable routines which might be formulated into natural
laws. One can always find a sufficient reason for the choice
that was made. Nothing is purely capricious. And yet as
one contemplates future action, he knows he is free, he feels
the pull of obligation. Even his retrospective analysis of behavior is always colored by the sense of guilt. The best objective evidence for this freedom is the uniform reliability of
juries in criminal trials where there is a question of responsibility. Clever defense attorneys, like the famous Clarence
Darrow, who made a practice of this, can always find determining factors in the crime situation which qualify the responsibility, but when the juryman is locked in the council
room he must decide the guilt or innocence and the degree
of responsibility on the basis of his own sympathetic feelings
of freedom were he put in like circumstances. So long as man

knows he is free, there is not much danger that counsels of pure determinism will rule the affairs of men.

Why should this situation be called a paradox? If there is freedom at all, then capricious causes can be expected. Nothing is certain! Anything can happen! Yet not everything does happen, and the possibilities for prediction are truly remarkable. On the other hand, if everything is determined by mechanical laws, then there is no responsibility or guilt. But these are both too vivid in the conscience of men. Nor does it seem very promising that the paradox can be resolved by carving out mutually exclusive spheres of freedom and determinism.

The exploration of this paradoxical situation and the hope of resolving it set Immanuel Kant to work on his critiques. The *Critique of Pure Reason* sought to establish the possibility and the limits of reason in making valid scientific judgments about the nature of the objective world given in experience. Then the *Critique of Practical Reason* affirmed the reality of freedom and sought to explore its nature in man's activities as an ethical person. A long list of books on the shelf of modern philosophy which explore the problem further will attest that Kant hardly resolved the paradox.

This is the modern form of a very ancient paradox. Pelagius ran into the same, in theological rather than scientific terms, when he went to Rome at the beginning of the fifth century and was shocked by the vices of the Christian community and the slipslop practices of religious education. He found a deep and gloomy pessimism about human nature and an exaggerated dependence on baptism to wash away the taint of original sin and guarantee the salvation of children. Small wonder, perhaps, when we remember that he was in Rome during the decade when the imperial city was under threat from the hordes of Alaric the Goth and that he escaped from there to Carthage when the city was sacked in 410 A.D. Pelagius taught that man is both free and by nature good and that God has not laid a moral obligation upon him which he is not capable of achieving. Therefore religious education is more important than sacraments, in fact, there is more than a suggestion that the latter might be dispensed with entirely if there is a temptation to use them for magical purposes.

The British monk clashed headlong with the greatest and most versatile mind among the Fathers who formulated the Christian tradition, the Bishop of Hippo, St. Augustine. In his earlier labors as defender of the faith, Augustine was confronted with the heresies of the Manichaeans, from which group he had entered the Christian fold. This was a doctrine not unlike some modern forms of determinism. Man's full responsibility was denied and sin was traced to external causes over which man has no control. Then the great debater produced a brilliant defense of freedom and responsibility.

When confronted with the Pelagian threat to the efficacy and necessity of the sacraments, Augustine was cast in the role of defender of the Church, and his formula for this was the inadequacy of man and his absolute dependence on God. The argument for "irresistible grace" was based on his own experience of rebellion and conversion, and in his case, at least, it would seem to be true. The doctrine of "prevenient grace" rationalizes one of the most significant aspects of Christian piety, intercessory prayer. This is the notion that an act of divine grace intervenes to turn the sinner toward God prior to any move of his own will, and if that is not true, why should we ever pray for others. We pray for others on the assumption that their redemption depends upon an initial act of God. Yet when the saint proclaimed the evangel in his preaching at the cathedral of Hippo, there is no indication that he did not make a forceful appeal to the free action of men.

This is the paradox of freedom and divine determinism, man's responsibility and God's foreknowledge and grace, a little different turn of the phrase from the modern paradox of mechanism and teleology. In the debates of the Middle Ages and the Reformation, the argument in that theological form was certainly exhausted, but the paradox can hardly be said to have been resolved once for all. Yet a kind of practical adjustment in Christian piety came about which now seems to be heartily endorsed by all parties to the traditional conflict. It appears in the practices of the Puritans, who theoretically embraced an absolute divine predestination and yet made themselves famous for works of piety and morality. Again a theoretical dilemma is met with a paradox of practical action. It is said of the Puritan that he prayed as though everything depended on God, and then worked as though everything depended on him. Do we need a new scientific Puritanism today, people who not only understand the mathematical patterns of atomic energy but accept the responsibilities of free moral men?

Pragmatism in the Book of Job

To turn back to the paradox of Job, we must recognize that neither the paradox in all its fulness is worked out there, nor is there a solution of the problem of evil. Basically the poem is neither a work in theology nor philosophy, but the spontaneous expression of practical piety. The humanistic interpretation of the work finds little that is significant beyond the arguments of the symposium. This overlooks entirely the way in which God reaches out for man, as portrayed in the book, but it must be admitted that this side of the paradox of religion does not reach a full statement until the New Testament doctrines of atonement and grace.

The religious spirit of man does not meet the evil of existence with a theodicy (using that term to mean a theoretical explanation of evil under the justice of God). Theodicies are the product of philosophy. The Book of Job shows the insufficiency of any mere philosophical theodicy. It contains a series of what may be called practical suggestions for adjustment which are typical of the way religion has always met the problem of evil. These are: belief in a judgment beyond death, the intrinsic value of moral integrity, the disciplinary value of suffering and its stimulus to human progress, and suffering as a pathway to God. These suggestions as a sort of pragmatic solution of the problem of evil will engage our attention in subsequent chapters. Next, however, we must take a look at the way our poets deal with the problem of death.

Chapter 7

DEATH AND BEYOND

According to Origen, the third-century theologian of Alexandria, it was a custom in the churches of his time to read the Book of Job during Passion Week. The New Testament, as we have it, was not then in use, and this Old Testament poem was recognized as a type of the passion of Christ, the mystery of the cross in daily life, and sign of the enmity between Christ and Satan. The practice would be eminently fitting, for no literature could be found to make the problem of passion and death more poignant.

But we must not forget that the book belongs to a pre-Christian era. Suffering and death take on a different meaning in the light of the Cross and Resurrection of Christ than they held for Job and the poets who told his tale. Among many moderns, the Christian hope has dimmed, and for these the book strikes a peculiar note of sympathetic feeling. Corliss Lamont opens his anthology of humanist poetry, *Man Answers Death*,[1] with quotations from Job and Lucretius.

The Gilgamesh Epic

A peculiar feeling about death appears in most ancient literature. There is none of the romantic feeling about it so common in modern poetry. The oldest epic poem in any language, the Gilgamesh Epic of ancient Babylonia, deals with death as its central problem. The earliest version be-

---

[1] Corliss Lamont (ed.), *Man Answers Death* (New York: G. P. Putnam's Sons, 1936).

longs to the Sumerian age, at least 2000 B.C. or before. On this question of death and beyond there are similarities and contrasts with the Book of Job which are significant.

Gilgamesh was king and legendary hero of ancient Uruk. The story opens with his oppressive rule, and the complaint of the people to the gods. As a relief they send Enkidu to be his companion and divert his attention. A wild and untamed creature, Enkidu appears first among the animals. A herdsman reports his presence, and a courtesan is sent to seduce and civilize him. She leads him to Gilgamesh and the two fall into a fierce struggle. After Gilgamesh finally lays Enkidu on his back, the two become fast friends and companions on many heroic exploits. The goddess of love, Ishtar, jealous of this diversion, undertakes to seduce Gilgamesh, but he cannot be won away from his new friend. She sends the bull of heaven against them and together the two slay the fierce animal. Ishtar appeals to the gods and a decree is given that one of the two must die. The lot falls on Enkidu and he is laid low by illness. Before his death, Enkidu recounts a dream which describes the underworld. Then Gilgamesh realizes his own mortality: "When I die, shall I not be like unto Enkidu?" His exploits are forgotten; no glory of the past can bring him comfort.

Gilgamesh then goes in search for the secret of immortality. He has heard of Utnapishtim, an ancient relative, the Babylonian Noah, who built a great ship and rode out the flood. When the waters receded, the gods made him and his wife and his boatman immortal. They dwell in the Isle of Bliss beyond the Western Mountains. After great hardship when passing through the desert, Gilgamesh arrives at the mountains to find the caverns guarded by fearsome dwarf men. They recognize Gilgamesh as part god and let him pass. Six days and seven nights he gropes through utter darkness and comes out by the Waters of Death. A goddess, in the person of a barmaid, tries to discourage him, but he finds the boatman of Utnapishtim who takes him across. This part of the epic has been called the earliest mortuary myth in the world.[2] Utnapishtim tells him that he must remain awake for six days and seven nights, but he immediately falls asleep for that length of time. What Gilgamesh learns for his trouble is the dictum of Aristotle with reference to Socrates that "all men are mortal." Disillusioned, he makes his way back to Uruk, resigned to his fate. Then, like Faust, he snatches a moment of comfort in satisfaction with self-accomplishment, for he had built the great wall around the city. By the help of favorable gods and magic the spirit of Enkidu is permitted to ascend and instruct Gilgamesh on the state of the dead in the realm below. On this sad and gloomy note the epic ends.

Gilgamesh had to discover his mortality after a long and bitter struggle. Death is not an immediate intuition of man but an inference from experience. We cannot even imagine our own death for we always survive as spectator. As Freud put the situation, "In the unconscious, every one of us is convinced of his immortality." [3] Ancient man entertained few doubts about his survival. According to the Book of Genesis, man was created immortal and death was imposed as a penalty for sin. In the lands surrounding the Hebrews, speculation on origins did not get so far, but survival was taken for granted. Disembodied spirits continue to exist in the underworld and are able to return to bless or plague the living. Their existence must be sustained by offerings of water, wine, food, and blood. Libations must be poured out continually and food must be left in the sepulchers. In the revelations of Enkidu to Gilgamesh, the number of sons which a man leaves determines his status below. In Mesopotamia and Egypt, the cult of the dead flourished for thousands of years before Job was written, and in Greece the state of the souls in

[2] W. F. Jackson Knight, Cumaean Gates (Oxford: Basil Blackwell, 1936), p. 18.

[3] Sigmund Freud, Civilization, War, and Death (London: Hogarth Press, 1939), p. 41.

Hades was always in thought. Elaborate and carefully per-
formed rites for the dead were required to insure safe passage
below, as we find illustrated in Homer's *Iliad*.

Early Hebrew Speculations

The strict monotheism which developed in the Holy Land
led to complete rejection of the cult of the dead. Excavations
indicate that in earlier times Hebrew burials may have included food offerings, though the evidence is not conclusive;
but even this seems not to have survived long. The notion
that spirits acquired supernatural powers, that they could influence affairs on earth, and that they must be propitiated,
was rejected, although in one notable passage the witch of
En-dor conjures up the shade of Samuel to plague Saul
(I Sam. 28). The king, however, was practicing a heathen
sorcery which his own decree had condemned.

It is sometimes said that the Jews did not believe in immortality but this must be carefully scrutinized. Nowhere
in the Old Testament do we find the doctrine of individual
immortality clearly stated. There are foregleams only of what
emerges in a full stream of light in apocalyptic literature and
becomes a fixed star in the firmament of the New Testament.
But they believed in survival of the spirit in Sheol, Hebrew
counterpart of the Babylonian underworld and the Greek
Hades. Their denials are simply denials that the spirits can
come back from the grave to this life. The dead are divested
of supernatural powers, and Sheol is stripped of that pantheon
of deities which rule the realm of the dead in surrounding
countries. Yahweh is God of the living and the dead. He is
the ruler of Sheol as well as of the heavens.

A factor which determined their thought, as we have seen
before, in addition to monotheism, was the strong national-
istic aspect of early prophetic religion. When a man died,
old and full of days, and was gathered to his fathers, he had

made his contribution. His hope was not in himself but in his family and tribe. Questioning reflection seems never to have been centered upon the destiny of the individual; only upon the destiny of the nation. The Chosen People were immortal. The nation would live forever, and be established upon Mount Zion, and to it all other peoples should be tributary. The prophetic writings set a strange atmosphere for us because few Christians ever think of their destiny as in any way connected with the future of the nation or even their church. That was a simple and circumscribed, though compact and morally profound, little world in which Hebrew culture developed. It came to a tragic end in the terrible calamities of marching empires: war, siege, and exile. Scattered abroad, the Jew came to stand alone as an individual. He possessed peculiar traditions which made him successfully resist amalgamation but that very resistance would have been impossible had the traditions not been sufficiently flexible to meet new and radically different conditions. In the postexilic period, speculations arose in Judah about the destiny of individuals.

None of these things made Job's problem easy, facing death as he thought. With these aspects of primitive faith suppressed and the more mature doctrines of resurrection and immortality not yet developed, death and the beyond took on a very dismal aspect. Death could hardly be called the central problem of the Book of Job as it was of the Gilgamesh Epic. In the face of the sufferings through which he passes, as the story unfolds, impending death is a promise of release. Yet no less than forty-five passages, comprising nearly one tenth of the book, deal with death. Job alternates between longing for release and portrayals of the dread and anxiety of it in words that are unmatched in the poetry of the world. The first passionate speech, cursing the day of his birth, ends in a cry for the grave:

> Why is light given to him that is in misery,
>   and life to the bitter in soul,
> who long for death, but it comes not,
>   and dig for it more than for hid treasures;
> who rejoice exceedingly,
>   and are glad, when they find the grave? (3:20-22)

And the fourteenth chapter of Job has carried man's deepest feeling of dread for two millennia:

> Man that is born of a woman
>   is of few days, and full of trouble.
> He comes forth like a flower, and withers;
>   he flees like a shadow, and continues not. (14:1-2)

Death is the "king of terrors" (18:14). It may strike suddenly as it did in the tornado which destroyed his children:

> Between morning and evening they are destroyed;
>   they perish for ever without any regarding it. (4:20)

Or death may linger and keep a man in prolonged suffering.

A "death wish" is also sharply stated in 6:8-10, but we do not have a case history which would justify all the implications of the term in Freudian psychology:

> O that I might have my request,
>   and that God would grant my desire;
> that it would please God to crush me,
>   that he would let loose his hand and cut me off!
> This would be my consolation;
>   I would even exult in pain unsparing;
>   for I have not denied the words of the Holy One. (6:8-10)

The word of his wife to "curse God, and die" might be interpreted as advice to commit suicide. To curse God would be equivalent, for in primitive belief God would surely strike one dead. But Job still takes comfort in the fact that he has not renounced God. He is not sure what he might do under the provocation of the debate, and so if death is inevitable, he hopes for it to come quickly and spare him that disgrace.

Rabbi Israel Gerber has discussed the implications of Job's death wish in an interesting book,[4] and he points out the reason why Job does not commit suicide. Misery and suffering alone seldom lead people to lay their hand on themselves. The one element necessary is a complete loss of self-esteem. They must be deserted by the superego, to put it in the technical terms of psychology. This is the one thing Job never lost; to the very end he holds fast his integrity.

The Hebrew Sheol

In the *Upanishads* of ancient India, death is identified with the primal hunger, the first being, out of which creation arises. Death is called death or hunger "because he eats everything." There is no underworld in the Indic literature. The spirits go on to an abode in the heavens beyond the Western Mountains where they are under the jurisdiction of the sky god, Varuna, pictured as a kindly and benevolent deity. Sickness and suffering are penance for sin, and there is an elaborate system of rewards and punishments involved in the doctrine of reincarnation. What the ancient Hindu dreads is not death as such but the necessity of return to life. Yet the feeling is felicitous compared to the dismal concept of the underworld among the Semites.

In the Gilgamesh Epic, the dead are pictured as feeding on dust when the food offerings run out. The notion of the dead's feeding had been abandoned in Israel, but dust is a familiar figure for death in Job.

> Remember that thou hast made me of clay;
> and wilt thou turn me to dust again? (10:9)

[4] Israel Joshua Gerber, *The Psychology of the Suffering Mind* (New York: The Jonathan David Co., 1951). This work is a psychological study of the Book of Job, with much suggestive material from the point of view of modern clinical and pastoral psychology. In 1950 I examined this book, then a doctoral dissertation, at Boston University.

where then is my hope?
    Who will see my hope?
  Will it go down to the bars of Sheol?
    Shall we descend together into the dust?
                            (17:15-16. Cf. 7:21; 34:15)

The poet does not make a clear distinction between death, the grave, and the abode of the dead, and he never draws the sharp contrast between the body and the spirit that is so familiar to us. Sheol is the Biblical word for the underworld, and it is a place of dust and darkness as it was in neighboring countries long before. Though early Hebrews did not give much thought to the afterlife, they still did not think of the grave as ending all. They believed in a continued story in Sheol. Pringle-Pattison remarks in his *The Idea of Immortality* [5] that

> It seems strange at first sight that the Jews, with their strongly ethical belief in Yahweh, should ever have been able to reconcile themselves to the gloomy heathen eschatology of Sheol.

He explains by the fact that the ethical and religious ideas of the nation centered in social immortality, as explained above. The Greeks were the first to moralize their concept of Hades, but the moralization went further among Jews and Christians after the doctrine of resurrection was established.

Sheol was very vivid to the Job poets. The name appears seven times in the text and no less than five other passages refer to the idea. It is described as "the Pit" (33:22), below the sea and down near the foundations of the earth (11:8; 26:5; 38:16-17). In this place of utter weakness, apathy, and gloom (10:21-22), the soul, in a sort of dream consciousness, without individuality, suffers the pangs of the body's decay. There is no distinction of good or bad in the Job Sheol; that

[5] Andrew Seth Pringle-Pattison, *The Idea of Immortality*, p. 17 (Oxford: Clarendon Press, 1922).

came later as we shall see. A. S. Peake in the New Century Bible commentary on Job [6] describes the existence thus:

> There the bloodless shades drag out an apathetic semblance of life, in a peace whose intolerable tedium could seem welcome relief only to the bitterest anguish.

And yet Job cries out to be hid in Sheol. There are two passages of special note in describing the place. One expresses a specific dread of the melancholy abode.

> "Why didst thou bring me forth from the womb?
>   Would that I had died before any eye had seen me,
> and were as though I had not been,
>   carried from the womb to the grave.
> Are not the days of my life few?
>   Let me alone, that I may find a little comfort
> before I go whence I shall not return,
>   to the land of gloom and deep darkness,
> the land of gloom and chaos,
>   where light is as darkness." (10:18-22)

But Sheol has one feature which, in his utter despair, gives Job a ray of comfort:

> There the wicked cease from troubling,
>   and there the weary are at rest.
> There the prisoners are at ease together;
>   they hear not the voice of the taskmaster.
> The small and the great are there,
>   and the slave is free from his master. (3:17-19)

The Vindicator

Whatever fault we may find with the friends of Job as counselors, they do make a signal contribution, not only by stating the orthodox doctrines as a foil, but by stimulating Job to progress. Friends who can keep quiet for seven days and seven nights without saying a word are not a total loss

---

[6] A. S. Peake, *Job* in the *New Century Bible* (Edinburgh: T. C. & E. C. Jack, 1904), pp. 8 ff.

as counselors.[7] For Job makes a very definite psychological progression in the drama. He starts the conversation with bitter resentment typical of a man in trouble, directed against God and fate. The sharp challenge of the friends gives him a relatively harmless object on which to vent his spleen. They are his enemies and they represent mankind in general. This likewise is typical of the counseling process. It relieves the tension. Rabbi Gerber finds in the poem the whole gamut of human emotions in the face of suffering: insecurity, anxiety, loneliness, alternation of goals, fantasy both in the form of night dreams and daydreams, deeper insight in resignation, ingenious logical devices in arguing away his guilt, fear, humility, hopelessness, need for sympathy, and anger. Job moves through these to prayer. The elegies are deeply sincere outpourings of a wounded heart. In spite of his protestations of innocence, these moments lead him into guarded words of repentance. He comes through with restored confidence in his own integrity, and subsides into silence from which he emerges with faith.

What Job and the poets are concerned about is not just the stamina equal to suffering. Death and the apathy of Sheol would afford release from that at least. The deeper concern is the moral question and the justice of God. What troubles them more deeply is the honor of man as a moral individual. One easy way to solve the problem, voiced by Job's friends and taken by some Christian theologians, is to deny that man has any honor. He is by nature sinful and can do no good. But laying aside the theological question, there is a human situation. Job's misfortunes are a sign in the eyes of the world that he is a vile sinner, not just a normal sinner because he is a creature, but since his sufferings are great, his wickedness must be great. The terror which grips him is the

---

[7] Dr. Gerber, op. cit., makes a valiant defense of Job's friends as counselors. There is an argument yet to be resolved among modern psychologists over the theory of good counseling. This is an important contribution.

dread that he will die and go down to Sheol with this stain upon his reputation, and he will not be able to return thither to set the matter right. The idea of such a return was not new, as we have seen, but the primitive ghost theory had been thoroughly rejected. Yet here it creeps in under a new form, a return not to plague his enemies but to attain knowledge of his vindication.

The insight begins at the end of the matchless elegy in the seventh chapter (7:21). After he is laid in the dust, God will grope for him in the dark abyss, but it will be too late for he will not be. The soul in Sheol is equivalent to that not-being which is yet included in being, according to Platonic philosophy (10:19). This seventh chapter has about it the quality which Kierkegaard was referring to when he said that "He who has learned rightly to be in dread has learned the most important thing."[8] For the Danish sage, one is surely bent for perdition either not to have known dread or to sink under it. Job has it and it starts him on the road to salvation.

If he could just be given the chance to plead his cause before God in person! He believes deep in his heart, in spite of his torrent of accusations against providence, that God is good, and that some horrible mistake has been made. Or, if an impartial umpire could be found to stand between him and God, the account might be adjusted. But such is not possible,

> For he is not a man as I am, that I might answer him,
>   that we should come to trial together.
> There is no umpire between us,
>   who might lay his hand upon us both. (9:32-33)

Despairing of ever seeing God himself, he pleads for a witness to vouch for him on high, and he finally rises to the positive assertion that a Vindicator lives to champion his cause. All this longing for vindication of his individual honor the poet places in the old Sheol concept:

[8] Sören A. Kierkegaard, The Concept of Dread (Princeton: Princeton University Press, 1946), p. 139.

Oh that thou wouldest hide me in Sheol,
    that thou wouldest conceal me until thy wrath be past,
    that thou wouldest appoint me a set time, and remember me!

It is a tremendous hope, and it leads to the eternal question,

If a man die, shall he live again?

O heavenly insight, O marvelous prospect!

All the days of my service I would wait,
    till my release should come.
Thou wouldest call, and I would answer thee;
    thou wouldest long for the work of thy hands.

For then thou wouldest number my steps,
    thou wouldest not keep watch over my sin;
my transgression would be sealed up in a bag,
    and thou wouldest cover over my iniquity. (14:13-17)

But the hope is a forlorn one. It is prefaced by one of the most incisive denials of immortality ever dictated by man's empirical judgment.

So man lies down and rises not again;
    till the heavens are no more he will not awake,
    or be roused out of his sleep. (14:12)

A glimmer of light, however, is not easily quenched after it has illuminated the inner soul. Man wavers between despair and hope. It flares up a little brighter the second time. He will die, but his blood will remain uncovered and will require a vindicator which will be forthcoming:

O earth, cover not my blood,
    and let my cry find no resting place.
Even now, behold, my witness is in heaven,
    and he that vouches for me is on high. (16:18-19)

God may be the cause of his sufferings but surely he will not leave the blot upon his reputation. In the heavenly councils there must be some witness on his behalf—a Vindicator as well as an Adversary.

A Disputed Passage

Finally the light breaks in a climactic flash in the nine-teenth chapter:

> Oh that my words were written!
>   Oh that they were inscribed in a book!
> Oh that with an iron pen and lead
>   they were graven in the rock for ever!
> For I know that my Redeemer lives,
>   and at last he will stand upon the earth;
> and after my skin has been thus destroyed,
>   then without my flesh I shall see God,
> whom I shall see on my side,
>   and my eyes shall behold, and not another.
> My heart faints within me! (19:23-27)

The word Redeemer may be translated Vindicator, as indicated in the footnotes of the revised versions. The above passage is quoted from the Revised Standard Version. But in the Vulgate and in the King James Version, which set the meaning for the Middle Ages in the first instance, and for the English-speaking world in the second, the reading is quite otherwise:

> For I know that my redeemer liveth, and that he shall stand at the latter day upon the earth: And though after my skin worms destroy this body, yet in my flesh shall I see God: Whom I shall see for myself, and mine eyes shall behold, and not an-other; though my reins be consumed within me.
>
> (King James Version)

Both affirm a resurrection faith, but the latter makes it mean what the idea of resurrection originally meant, a resurrection of the body. The Hebrew scholars tell us that this passage, transmitted by many scribes, is a very "corrupt text." This means that the various manuscripts are in disagreement and that the verses require emendation for clear meaning. It is doubtful that scholars can ever be sure what the original poem exactly stated. The reason is that from the beginning the resurrection has been much disputed, and disputes over doctrine are notorious corruptors of ancient texts.

Many suggestions for emendation and translation may be found in the vast literature on the passage. Still the question is an important one, and so the translations of two very recent scholars may be cited. Alexander Heidel, in his translation of the Gilgamesh Epic and study of the Old Testament parallels,[9] produced at the Oriental Institute of the University of Chicago, gives the following version with a thorough exposition of the textual difficulties:

> But I know: My Redeemer lives, and at the last will He arise on the dust. And behind my skin, now thus struck to pieces, and that from out of my flesh, I shall behold God, whom I shall behold for my good, and mine own eyes shall see Him and that not as another. My reins fail with longing in my bosom.

The poet was working earnestly with the idea of Job's vindication. The shredded skin of the man is the badge of his condemnation. His heart and sense of justice demand removal of the blot. It obviously cannot come before his impending death. The hope of vindication beyond gradually creeps up on him. It must be a very personal experience or it would be meaningliness. His own eye must see the Vindicator, and not as a stranger. But how could this be conceived apart from the flesh? If one will examine all instances in the book where flesh, spirit, or soul are used, he will see that they are very close together, almost interchangeable. There is no intimation of the existence of a disembodied spirit. Only once in the Old Testament, for that matter, is there such a suggestion, referred to above: the raising of the shade of Samuel to speak to Saul. The word flesh has a personal connotation. When the glory of the Lord shall be revealed, to take one familiar instance, "all flesh shall see it together"

[9] Alexander Heidel, *The Gilgamesh Epic and Old Testament Parallels* (Chicago: The University of Chicago Press, 1946), p. 211.

(Isa. 40:5). There is none of that sharp split between the flesh and the spirit which came to figure in New Testament thought. If such a resurrection experience can be conceived at all, it would more likely be "from out of my flesh."

The passage has always been taken as a simple affirmation, but Edward D. Kissane, another recent author of a commentary on Job,[10] offers the novel suggestion that the verses should be rendered as a conditional proposition:

> And I know that my Defender liveth,
>   And the Eternal will stand forth on the dust;
> And after my skin is stripped off, did I but see Him,
>   Without my flesh were I to behold God,
> He whom I should see would be on my side,
>   And whom my eyes should behold would not be strange.

This has the virtue of making the passage more consistent with the skepticism of Job in other speeches if consistency is a virtue. Most modern commentators who question this passage and want to deny its implications for the doctrine of immortality are moved not simply by the textual difficulties but by the notion that it must thus be made consistent. But the actual situation of man is more truly such an alternation between hope and despair, often of the most extreme sort, and the genius of great literature is its vivid portrayal of that human ambivalence.

We shall have to wait for the linguistic specialists to decide whether Job said the manifestation of his Vindicator would come with his flesh and skin restored or without them. This would seem to be a very positive affirmation, nonetheless, even though the exact form is hidden in uncertainty, as, indeed, all affirmations of experience beyond must be.

If this is a statement of faith in the physical resurrection, it would probably be the earliest declaration of the idea in

[10] Edward D. Kissane, *The Book of Job* (New York: Sheed & Ward, 1946). Quotation from p. 114 ff., comment on p. 121.

literature. The unclear statement of it would favor that sup-
position. Later it took firm hold of Jewish and early Christian thought. In clear detail it appears in Isaiah 26:19. Some
think this is the earliest statement of it. Sheol, in this little
apocalypse of Isaiah, has become the pit of punishment for
the wicked (24:22), and the righteous shall be resurrected to
reward. The same concept is found in Psalms 16, 49, and 73,
and in Daniel 12:2. All these are generally assigned to a
later date than the Book of Job. In the apocalyptic books
which appeared just before the New Testament period, the
doctrine received much elaboration and it was never called
into question by the apostles (cf. Acts 23:6).

This nineteenth chapter strikes a climax toward which all
the action and dialogue of the first part of the drama move,
but it is a pinnacle upon which a writer of that period could
not abide. Job returns to the lowlands immediately, and,
as C. F. Kent says, "threshes out the problem entirely in the
arena of man's earthly existence." [11] While such words of an
ancient poet about Sheol and a Vindicator do not give us the
doctrine of immortality as such, nor any thing in the way of
proofs, yet their value lies in the fact that so long ago, before
the Christian faith had filled the idea full of significant
meaning, there arose such an expression of the natural faith
of man. Whenever men have fallen into complete denial, it
would seem to be a rationalization of despair.[12] It recalls
some familiar lines of Tennyson:

[11] Charles F. Kent, The Growth and Contents of the Old Testament
(New York: Chas. Scribner's Sons, 1926).

[12] See, for example, a very interesting recent work by Curtis Reynolds
called Suicide Note (Los Angeles: New Age Publishing Co., 1948). On
page 56 he says: "From a standpoint of what seems to be normal human
reasoning, as inaccurate as it might be, it is easier for me to have faith that
life is a form of rust growing on the mysterious machine of nature. I cannot believe that there is an all-powerful God who deliberately made us what
we are."

Whatever crazy sorrow saith,
No life that breathes with human breath
Has ever truly long'd for death.

'T is life, whereof our nerves are scant,
O, life, not death, for which we pant;
More life, and fuller, that I want.
(From *The Two Voices*)

Chapter 8

THE PRAGMATIC IMPORTANCE
OF SURVIVAL

In the last analysis, our faith in survival beyond death will depend upon our philosophy of life, upon the place which we conceive man to hold in the universal scheme of things. If our philosophy comprehends a universe with friendly purposes toward the self-conscious denizens of earth, if man is created in the image of God and for purposes of free moral achievement, then human values are ultimate in reality, and man's subconscious intuition of immortality, as Freud thought of it, presents a coherent basis for faith; but if we come to look upon the universe as indifferent or hostile to human values, and if we think human personality represents no absolute worth in the scheme of things, then belief in immortality becomes irrational and perhaps impossible.

This is a phase of belief where dogmatism must be assiduously avoided. No verification of survival is available beyond the coherence of reason and faith. Perhaps that is to say that dogmatism should be avoided with regard to all our beliefs because there is no higher verification than coherence for any of them. Whether or not we believe in immortality certainly makes a difference in our religion; it is probably the main decisive difference today between religious humanism and orthodox Christianity. Ancient Hebrew religion and ethics and early Buddhism have shown the possibility of what Walter Lippmann in *Preface to Morals*[1] called "high

[1] Walter Lippmann, *Preface to Morals* (New York: The Macmillan Co., 1929).

religion," that is, religion without belief in immortality; and what might be called "low religion" is represented by many forms of Christianity and other world religions which cultivate superstitious fears of the gods and the hereafter. It was such a low religion in paganism which gave rise to the first naturalistic rejection of religion by Epicurus and Lucretius.

In Christianity the development of the doctrine of resurrection has been a natural concomitant of its individualism and personalism, its insistence upon the absolute worth of the individual soul. This cannot be lightly cast aside as a mere rationalization of desire. All thinking is heavily motivated by human desires, even scientific thinking. A rationalization is invalid only when it is demonstrated to be irrational rationalization. There is, of course, an element of circularity in any moral argument for immortality. It goes like this: the permanence of value requires immortality, and values are values just because they are permanent. Such circularity inheres in any argument from coherence within a system. Religion, at any rate, posits a set of values as the ultimate in the universe, and then finds the hope of immortality a very practical help in facing the denial of those values in experience.

The antithesis is the thesis of naturalism that all values belong only to human experience on earth and end with death. William E. Hocking in his *Thoughts on Death and Life* [2] subjects this claim to careful scrutiny and counters with the dictum that duration is a dimension of value. This puts the matter on the basis of the spirit of pragmatism, that judgments of reality must be grounded on judgments of value. He concludes:

> The notion of survival has no direct empirical standing, no place in the business of science. In philosophy, it is a last chapter, an appendix, a footnote to other matters. Just on this

[2] William E. Hocking, *Thoughts on Death and Life* (New York: Harper & Bros., 1937), p. 112.

account, for human life in the concrete, that is to say, for religion, it is the most important of all dogmas.

A religious dogma is an affirmation of faith, but "dogmatic
certainty" is something else, and it would seem to be impossible in this case, both on account of literary skepticism,
like that in the Book of Job, and what modern scientific
knowledge has done to the ancient concepts of space and
time. It is not so easy to locate hell or heaven as in the time
of Dante or Milton. Our world is not an independent unit,
layered or storied to suit a human judgment of value, from
lowest hell for Satan to highest heaven for saints and deity.
Motion is circular; there are no straight lines, and no absolutely fixed point of reference; and, therefore, no up or down.
Yet the enlargement of cosmic speculations does not limit
the imagination. There are both microcosmic and macro-
cosmic realms which the ancients never dreamed of. Heaven,
hell, purgatory, and many intermediate stages might easily
be located, so long as we remember that the concepts are
poetic. No scientific proofs or disproofs are available. The
darkened veil is drawn, and no one has returned from thence;
no unquestioned means of communication has yet been
devised. Even Jesus had astonishingly little to say about the
the realm beyond; but there is infinite promise in his word
that "where I am you may be also."

Rewards and Punishments

The idea of survival may have originated among primitive
peoples in dream experience, but it was the possibility of
rewards and punishments which carried the conception to
its final development. It makes possible a pragmatic solution
of the problem of evil. Job's cry for vindication is an open-
ing phase of that speculation. The next step among the Jews
was the idea of a resurrection of the righteous from Sheol to
receive a reward in heaven. The Greek separation of the
dead in Hades according to merit was another initial stage.

The demands of an abstract justice in God's rule are seen

in the orthodox theories of Job's three friends. The accounts must be balanced. This is a very persistent doctrine of all religion, where the idea of God is moralized at all. If man is free, then his life cannot be coerced here on earth; he may pursue the evil if he wills, but, as Plato puts the matter in the tenth book of the *Republic*, as soon as man moves beyond he is confronted by Necessity, who takes over, and all accounts are squared. The wicked flourish like the green bay tree, while Job lies on the ash heap full of boils. Surely this cannot be.

It was the demand of such a doctrine and the determination to work out the matter within the limitations of the old Hebrew faith which undoubtedly led the Job writers to finish off with the epilogue. After Job's bitter trial and submission to the Almighty, his family and friends come back to him with presents; his former wealth is restored doublefold, and seven new sons and three more beautiful daughters are born to him. He lives to see four generations of his family and dies old and full of days. Thus the orthodox solution of the problem of evil is saved. The only flaw is that it does not square with the facts of life. It is in a worse situation than the doctrine of rewards and punishments beyond, for that idea, though not confirmed, is not contradicted by experience.

But the idea of punishments beyond runs into a difficulty. Sensitive men must recognize as sin the vivid imprecations upon enemies, such as we have in some of the Psalms, and even in Job 20 and 21. When this goes into visions of eternal torment, the matter is even more in question. There is an interesting touch of this in the Slavonic Book of the Secrets of Enoch. Facing the terrible guardians of the gates of hell, Enoch says:

> Would that I had not seen you nor heard of your doings, and that those of my race had never come to you! Now they have only sinned a little in this life, and always suffer in eternal life. (XLII)

Among Christians the problem has always been troublesome, especially when hell is reserved for nonbelievers. The late George A. Gordon, eminent New England divine, was disturbed about the myriads of people past and present who stand before the Lord "bereft of moral grandeur," the vast plodding mass upon whose backs the labor of the world rests, the hordes of primitives, and men of early civilizations, "numerous as clouds of insects in summer heat," who "struggled, suffered, lived, loved, and hoped and died." "They are unfit for moral bliss, they are too many for doom." He found consolation in the word of Revelation, "And I saw the dead, small and great, stand before God." [3]

When Jesus in the Sermon on the Mount said,

> Love your enemies and pray for those who persecute you, so that you may be sons of your Father who is in heaven; for he makes his sun rise on the evil and on the good, and sends rain on the just and on the unjust,

he was doing more than abrogating the old Semitic law of "an eye for an eye and a tooth for a tooth." He was modifying the traditional orthodoxy of retributive justice. The attitude of Jesus toward enemies reveals the perfection of God in mercy and grace. When we apply this to immortality, much of the idea of retribution becomes patently absurd. If one has an enemy on earth, what benefit would it be in heaven to see him forever in torment? To take pleasure in it would be to place himself in jeopardy of hell.

Possibilities in Moral Achievement

The afterlife is often conceived in terms of a sharp dualism between the here and the hereafter, between time and eternity, or between the struggle and change of mortal toil and the saint's everlasting rest. The contrast reflects the

[3] In a sermon delivered at Old South Church, Boston, in 1916. Published by Pilgrim Press.

traditional distinction between appearance and reality, finite and infinite, change and identity. But it has become increasingly difficult to conceive the ultimate as static substance or established and unchanging completeness. Everywhere the universe presents itself as energy and activity, and fixed thinghood or substance as such always eludes. This may be due to our finiteness and mortality, subject to correction when the corruptible puts on incorruptibility; yet the elusiveness of a static world casts doubt upon its existence.

If the whole faith in immortality rests upon the status of values and persons, then it must be remembered that persons are known only in the character of growth. A heavenly bliss conceived as a reward for activity past and ended with this life is cast in the form of an excessive hedonism. An asceticism which denies itself the pleasures of normal life compensates by visions of otherworldly bliss. The error in the view is that pleasure is never anything but a by-product of successful activity. Values must be attained and measured by coherent functioning. This difficulty led the Scholastics, under the influence of Aristotle's rationalism, to picture the highest life both in earth and heaven as contemplation, an activity cultivated by philosophers. A static doctrine of immortality has been one item in the "narcotic types of religion" which needs to be corrected by a more activistic conception. In the case of Job it was the moral will which required vindication beyond. Immortality is an achievement both here and beyond.

Epicurus, who taught in Greece during the first half of the third century B.C., saw the idea of retribution in Hades, cultivated by the popular pagan cults, clustered with fears and superstitions which were a handicap to the free enjoyment of natural living and therefore an evil in itself. He sought to liberate his disciples from this blight by teaching a materialistic doctrine which denied all immortal survival, and by cultivating a rational and disciplined enjoyment of natural pleasures. Isolated individuals have, perhaps, demonstrated some nobility in this program; when adopted by Roman patrician society, and on a popular scale in much modern society, what it demonstrates is something else. There is a better way: free the idea of immortality of its fearbreeding superstitions so that it can serve as a vehicle for faith in the reality and eternity of value. Yet it must be recognized that when man becomes adequately aware of sin and the depravity of the human spirit, the notion of retribution cannot be entirely eradicated. At any rate, Christian thought carries Job's faith in moral vindication to faith in the permanent possibility of moral achievement.

An Argument for Survival

Death is not just the bringing of something to an end. It belongs in time to every instant—it is a function or dimension of time. What I was a moment ago died the instant that it was past. Time moves and the past can never be restored to existence. It is dead. But the fact that we are self-conscious beings enables us to transcend time to some extent. We can grasp the past in recollection. We are not limited to existence in time as an endless flow of instants. In the "now" we experience a span, which can be extended greatly, into the past by recollection and into the future by anticipation and prediction.

What my friend was the last time I saw him is now dead; so is that "I" which saw and talked with him; but the dead past can be resurrected both by him and by me in recollection. Our friendship depends upon this continual resurrection. This gives a kind of immortality to mutual love. But friendship also depends on anticipation that we shall deepen our feeling of community when we get together again. We look forward to the next meeting with joy. Then when the moment comes that he passes from my sight into the grave, as Enkidu passed from Gilgamesh, and I no longer have that anticipation, then death takes on its deepest meaning. I can still resurrect my friend in memory. At least to the end of my conscious life he will have a kind of immortality, but without the element of anticipation it is a very shadowy reality.

Ever since the writing of Saint Augustine's *Confessions*, these reflections on time and consciousness have been applied to deity and immortality. Consciousness transcends time because past, present, and future are meaningful only to a person who grasps them in experience. The meaning of real time is constituted by this transcendence. There is no past for an entity which does not have a mind capable of grasping it. The time which is measured by a series of marks on a dial of the clock, or by a tick of its mechanism, is an abstraction. It is given concrete reality in the form of duration for the person who views and interprets the dial or the ticks. Things, like the body, which have no consciousness still exist in time and are limited to it. They exist at each passing instant. They existed in the past, too, but not a past for themselves. That past is available only to the transcending conscious experience of an observer or user of these things. Each separate material thing which we see or touch has a beginning; it runs through a series of instants and it comes to an end. If there is any unchanging substance in them, it has so far eluded even the ultramicroanalysis of science. It, too, is an abstraction. Time is real because change is real, but the full meaning of time is in the time-spanning grasp of it by conscious experience.

The same would hold for the experience of identity. You are the same person at this hour today that you were at a like hour yesterday, or a month ago, or a year ago; and yet you are not the same. Incalculable change has taken place in you, your body, your thought, your environment, your experience; but you have a unique identity which belongs to your powers of recollection, that is, your ability for time transcendence. Such are the multiplicity and rapidity of the changes in the things of this world that identity cannot reside in their substance as stuff. They have identity as they proceed to fulfil purposes or functions of an overarching insight of some sort, a sort which is capable of time grasping. Only conscious persons have this ability, so far as we know.

This distinction between the meaning of time as a flow of instants, and time as duration through past, present, and future, is the best evidence for the stable distinction between things and persons or between body and soul. It would seem to indicate that conscious persons or souls are at least as real as time, and that past, present, and future of the world, real duration in other words, depends on the transcendent consciousness of God. A missing link in this chain of analogical reasoning, however, is the experience of duration for any finite person beyond the death of the body. We shall have to wait and see. Death will be momentary in finite time. Belief in immortality is the anticipation of ultimate time transcendence. Resurrection will be achievement.

Immortality or Resurrection

Historically, this argument goes back to Plato's demonstration in the Meno. An untrained slave boy is questioned by Socrates to draw from him a recognition of abstract mathematical concepts. This is interpreted as "recollection" on his part of rational ideas which are innate in his mind from a pre-existent state of the soul. If pre-existent, then the soul should transcend time at the future dimension. Plato's arguments for immortality supported the notion of survival for a disembodied soul, which, as we have seen, was a popular belief in the pagan world; but about that time there arose the materialist school at Abdera out of which came the Epicurean denial.

The concrete personalism of the Hebrew tradition, which did not make the sharp distinction between soul and body, gave birth to the unique doctrine of resurrection, and this should be carefully distinguished from the immortality of the Greek tradition. There is no rational argument for resurrection. It is miracle pure and simple. Its belief rests entirely on revelation. The Christian tradition, from Augustine on, adopted Plato's argument for the immortality of the soul and imposed upon it the revealed dogma of resurrection.

Discussions of the subject today are mixed and equivocal. The idealistic tradition in philosophy, which has been very strong in modern theology, follows the Platonic line, very often rejecting the idea of resurrection entirely. Yet modern philosophies, both idealistic and realistic, have tended to abolish the dualism between soul and body. That can be done by reducing body to mind or by reducing mind to body. Or there is a third way which is very popular now, and more in harmony it would seem with the ancient Hebrew thought, of making the two organic to each other, interdependent and inseparable. Both modern personalism and modern naturalism share this emphasis on organism. It would also seem that if the idea of immortality is to be preserved, it must carry some concept of resurrection. Both the dualism and the idealism which stem from Greek philosophy are unsatisfactory. But naturalism in the main tends to skepticism on survival just because of the rational difficulty about resurrection or the separation of soul and body. Under the form of religious humanism, as represented, for instance, in the works of Max Otto discussed in Chapter 6, it is aggressive in its denials and search for a philosophy of life under purely human categories. Personalists proceed from the principle that the inner activity of the conscious and subconscious person constitutes the key to reality, and perforce the concept of immortality is compatible. They rely on the value argument; life is prior to logic for them. Most of them probably reject the dogma of physical resurrection, but make the compromise which St. Paul did with Greek thought when he spoke of a "spiritual body" (I Cor. 15).

The equivocal feeling of the modernist, perhaps whatever his philosophical persuasion, is very well stated in the beautiful sonnet [4] of Irwin Edman entitled "Eternity":

> I know there is no meaning in the mist
> That wraps in gray these mountain girdled shores,
> Nor in these loud black waves once moonlight kissed,
> I fear no threat in their untimely roar.
> I cannot read a language in the surge
> Of breakers: there is no immortal sign
> In midnight winds: I hear no Demiurge
> Hiss in the storm, nor think the wind divine.
> I am too lessoned in the changeless law
> Behind the beauty of this cloud banked gloom,
> To mark in it with simple trembling awe,
> God's reckless accents of avenging doom.
>> Yet while thus Reason routs these dreams and fears,
>> Eternity keeps thundering in my ears.

Werfel and Kafka

The problem of modern European man in facing death is dramatically portrayed in two recent novels by European writers which deal with it. In *Embezzled Heaven*,[5] Franz Werfel has given the orthodox Christian solution of it.

Death makes sudden invasion of the home of a very modern family in the Bavarian Alps by a fall on the mountain side. The only son lies in an upstairs room, and the family is completely stunned, without knowledge even of the traditional customs for disposal of the dead. They sit petrified. The head of the house puts the thesis of the book:

[4] Reprinted from *Poems* by Irwin Edman (New York: Simon & Schuster, Inc., 1925).

[5] Franz Werfel, *Embezzled Heaven* (New York: The Viking Press, 1940), p. 117.

"Do you know why we men of the modern age are such godfor-saken, miserable creatures? We are on excellent terms with life, on loathsomely excellent terms. . . . But with its opposite in that room upstairs we don't know how to get on at all, my dear Theo, none of us, not one. . . ."

A pious and elderly servant, the cook of many years in the family, takes over. She knows exactly what to do precisely because she does not belong to this modern generation. She possesses not only a mastery of ancient folkways but the medieval faith as well.

The main part of the book is the story of this woman's life. All her savings and hopes for heaven have been invested in a nephew, ostensibly to put him through school and establish him in the priesthood. But he turns out to be an embezzler. When she retires and goes to visit him, she learns that his beautiful letters have been a fabrication of lies, and when she finds him living in utter sinfulness and degradation in a very modern city her heaven evaporates. It is a parable on what has happened to modern European society. Her Utopian heaven on earth has been embezzled by a modern urban culture.

Werfel's solution is a pilgrimage back to the philosophy of the Middle Ages—a Protestant orthodoxy might be put into similar terms. Joining a caravan to the Holy City, his heroine finds a splendid young priest, trained in the inspiring beauties and assuring faith of Scholasticism, guide to the party. He assumes the role of her absconded nephew in her dreams. After the visit to St. Peter's and the blessing of the Holy Father, she is ready for the bliss of the medieval heaven. Her young priest administers the last sacrament.

Two novels by Franz Kafka better represent the modern mood and in some ways recapture the atmosphere of the Book of Job. The Trial,[6] which deals with the problem of death, is the strange story of a bank official who is suddenly arrested

---

[6] Franz Kafka, The Trial (New York: Alfred A. Knopf, Inc., 1937).

and charged with crimes which are never specified. He is permitted to go about his business but must appear frequently for hearings in a strange court. The officers behave in queer and vague ways. A great many people are involved; apparently, in one way or another, everybody is involved. The law is never laid on the line. "K.," as the central figure is known—he is no hero—is presumed innocent, at least since the charges are never clearly specified, and yet he behaves in a way which indicates a haunting sense of guilt—just as any of us would under similar circumstances. Then, gradually, it dawns on the reader that the trial is the ordeal of life itself; the charge is the violation of the enigmatic moral law of the universe; the feeling is that which grips the hearts of all men facing judgment. The court is the social judgment of mankind, with a vague hierarchy of beings beyond reach, before which man never comes to stand until final judgment is passed. There is a poignant longing, like that of Job, to stand before God and plead one's cause before execution is carried out.

K. frantically searches for help. Friends do not come to him as they came to Job because he is not on an ash heap—he is modern man fighting for spiritual life in the midst of the choking billows of daily affairs. The men he seeks out only put him off with equivocal words designed to keep man struggling on to the end, but never lead him to freedom. The women take him to their arms, all but one who eludes him and becomes his main desire. While there are emotional comforts for the moment, they only lead him deeper into the involvment of guilt. The problem of the book is that of St. Paul's struggle with sin under the law. In the end, sentence of death is passed and K. is executed in a kind of dream experience which might be the accompaniment of any form of death.

The unfinished work, The Castle,[7] is a companion novel

---

[7] Franz Kafka, The Castle (New York: Alfred A. Knopf, Inc., 1930).

in which trust and the reality of grace are presented as the solution of life's problem in a universe which is hopelessly irrational.

A Personal Testimony

As I have read through the Book of Job with special attention to the passages concerning death and the beyond, I have reflected on the comparison with the way I face the problem today. Perhaps this is too personal, at least private, and not to be taken as representative of any school. We have an assurance in the Christian faith which was not available to Job, and yet I can hardly say that it has easily solved the enigma for me.

In younger years I was impressed with the arguments which would put something of a rosy hue on death. It is the way of nature, and under romantic tutelage, nature is supposed to be beautiful. If there were no death, there must soon be an end of birth, for the earth would not sustain the people. If there is birth, childhood, youth, and growth, and progress, then there must be an end to the individual that others may have their day. From the general point of view, death seems essential and valuable. But there is no "general value." Value and suffering lie only in the individual consciousness. For the individual who must face the grim reaper alone the question is seen from a different point of view. To him it is the undertaker's workshop, not the painted corpse and cut flowers of the chapel. Now, as I look down the long road occasionally, I can see death lurking in the shadows, and the picture is just about as fearsome as any poet or painter ever pictured it. Much modern poetry deals with death, and of all of it, the poem which strikes the most responsive feeling in this comparative reflection is the "Dirge Without Music" [8] by Edna St. Vincent Millay:

[8] Edna St. Vincent Millay, *The Buck in the Snow* (New York: Harper & Bros., 1928).

I am not resigned to the shutting away of loving hearts in the
    hard ground.
So it is, and so it will be, for so it has been, time out of mind:
Into the darkness they go, the wise and the lovely. Crowned
With lilies and with laurel they go; but I am not resigned.

Lovers and thinkers, into the earth with you.
Be one with the dull, the indiscriminate dust.
A fragment of what you felt, of what you knew,
A formula, a phrase remains,—but the best is lost.

The answers quick and keen, the honest look, the laughter,
    the love,—
They are gone. They are gone to feed the roses. Elegant and
    curled
Is the blossom. Fragrant is the blossom. I know. But I do not
    approve.
More precious was the light in your eyes than all the roses of
    the world.

Down, down, down into the darkness of the grave
Gently they go, the beautiful, the tender, the kind;
Quietly they go, the intelligent, the witty, the brave.
I know. But I do not approve. And I am not resigned.

Understanding without resignation is the mood both of
Job and the modern man. Epicurus sought by understanding of scientific truths to liberate the spirit from fears of
death so that pleasure might be unalloyed. But that is the
type of resignation which is not available to me, for two
reasons: first, there is no certainty that matter and motion are
all there is and that death is the end; nothing would seem
to be less certain in scientific and philosophical wisdom today than a materialistic metaphysics. Second, the possibility
of extinction is even more dreadful than judgment. I dread
the taking of an anesthetic or any drug which interferes with
normal consciousness. It is good to sleep because of the
confidence one has of awakening. In sleep the senses are
alert for any unusual disturbance. Anesthesia negates this
anticipation, especially the habitual use of narcotics. The

Freudian death wish is supposed to work itself out either in aggressiveness or in pathological tendencies to jeopardize life, of which the desire for oblivion is one form. Alcohol has an anesthetic effect which at initial stages opens the mind to certain forms of excitement, for some even an exaltation followed by depression; but it is a great hazard just because there is an enticing downward path from that to the oblivion of drunkenness, and the very unsatisfactoriness of life which makes man want the moment of exaltation will also favor the desire for oblivion. I simply do not understand narcotic addiction or oblivion drunkenness. Since one can never say that he is free from these Freudian complexes, that, perhaps, means that my adjustment to the death wish is no more beneficial. But to get back to Epicurus, one of the defects of our hedonism today is that we want the Epicurean way of life without metaphysics, and our uncertainty robs us of that peace of mind necessary to true pleasure and happiness. Our search for pleasure only leads us deeper into involvements in guilt.

A few years ago I spent a day with my father when the doctors pronounced a sentence of death upon him, with a dim hope of a stay of execution by surgery. As he prepared for the uncertain ordeal, his thoughts were on his children and his hopes for his grandchildren, and there was no loss of his usual cheerfulness. He accepted the consolations of religion with the same calmness and confidence with which he had always gone to the altar for the holy communion; it was no last-minute preparation, but the genuine pattern for the Christian accepting death. It is no exclusive possession of the Christian. I never think of this incident without remembering that scene of moral grandeur at the end of Plato's *Phaedo*, set in the Athenian jail when Socrates drank the hemlock on the decree of the state: the rational exploration of the immortal hope at an end, with inimitable wit the emotional disquietude of the gathered friends and the jailer are assuaged as he drinks, walks about until his legs begin to feel stiff, and lies down to await the end in silence. Then, rising a bit, he speaks to one of the group: "Crito, I owe a cock to Asclepius; will you remember to pay the debt?"

But out of the midst of health and lively work I am not able to look at death so calmly. It is not that I need vindication, nor assurance of reward, nor even that I fear punishment in the ordinary sense. The mercy of the Lord is about the most vivid religious conviction. Long ago I rejected the fires of hell as ground either for faith or ethics. But getting rid of the medieval hell has not solved modern man's anxiety. What I fear is something of the fate of Dives (Luke 16), for I have had so much of ease and good things this side of the veil, and there are so many beggars full of sores lying about in the world. It is a sort of Kierkegaardian dread which betokens original sin, not entirely washed away in baptism; or the anxiety of Kafka, the modern Jew, confronting life under the law. What fills me with such dread is the thought of judgment which we all must face if those accounts are squared. To stand revealed, with the books open, fills me with a dread which the assurance of grace and mercy have not yet erased.

But immortality is no certainty. It is an alternation of yes and no. Vague hopes, and human standards of justice, and a long past historical revelation, and even the metaphysical speculations about the nature of time and consciousness are not evidence for certainty; they are grounds for a lively and pragmatic faith only. With Tennyson I am willing to trust the larger hope.

> My own dim life should teach me this,
>   That life shall live for evermore,
>   Else earth is darkness at the core
> And dust and ashes all that is. (*In Memoriam*, xxxiv)

The ancient poet's protest finds a thousand echoes in modern literature. It was a wondrous and marvelous universe that

Job lived in, but one in which man could too easily be brought to disaster. What means all the chromatics of sunset, the splendor of starry firmament, the silvery glow of moonlight, the flash of snow-crowned mountains, the joys of home life, or the thrill of sitting in the gates of the world's affairs if conscious man can be so soon cut off in the midst of contemplation?

For the Christian, no other solution of the problem can take the place of the simple faith of Saint Paul:

> None of us lives to himself,
>   and none of us dies to himself.
> If we live, we live to the LORD,
>   and if we die, we die to the LORD;
> so then, whether we live or whether we die,
>   we are the LORD's. (Rom. 14:7-8)

Chapter 9

"THE INTEGRITY OF YOUR WAYS YOUR HOPE"

The pagan poet Lucretius saw with great clearness and stated with brilliant eloquence the situation of man. Even though his naturalism is in sharp contrast to Christian thought, he exhibits both the beauty and the failure of the detached and Epicurean view of life. He opens the second book of *De Rerum Natura* with these words:

> It is sweet, when on the great sea the winds trouble its waters, to behold from land another's deep distress; not that it is a pleasure and delight that any should be afflicted, but because it is sweet to see from what evils you are yourself exempt. It is sweet also to look upon the mighty struggles of war arrayed along the plains without sharing yourself in the danger. But nothing is more welcome than to hold the lofty and serene positions well fortified by the learning of the wise, from which you may look down upon others and see them wandering all abroad and going astray in their search for the path of life, see the contest among them of intellect, the rivalry of birth, the striving night and day with surpassing effort to struggle up the summit of power and be masters of the world. O miserable minds of men! O blinded breasts! in what darkness of life and in how great dangers is passed this term of life whatever its duration! not choose to see that nature craves for herself no more than this, that pain hold aloof from the body, and she in mind enjoy a feeling of pleasure exempt from care and fear? [1]

This passage is more notable for its statement of the vicissitudes of man in the midst of existence than it is for a solution.

[1] From Munro's translation in W. J. Oates (ed.), *The Stoic and Epicurean Philosophers* (New York: Random House, Inc., 1940).

Nothing is more vivid in the history of literature than the pessimism which overtook the Epicureans in their devotion to pleasure. No man, not even the philosopher or the poet, can take to the ivory tower and remain there for life. The realization of this makes the work of the Hebrew poets the more profound.

All Biblical religion, whether Jewish or Christian, is ethical. This means that what man does with his life, how he behaves as a moral being, and the responsibility he takes in his society have an integral bearing upon his relation to God and his hope of salvation. For this reason the Law is central to Judaism and the ethics of the New Testament is essential to the Christian faith. Nowhere is this more evident or more sharply posed as a problem than in the Book of Job. Job's moral integrity is both his ground of hope and a source of his despair.

Another pagan philosopher, Plato, and one of the Greek poets, make integrity the ground of man's hope. In discussing the question of old age in the first book of the *Republic*, he says:

> To him who is conscious of no sin, sweet hope, as Pindar charmingly says, is the kind nurse of his age: "Hope," he says, "cherishes the soul of him who lives in justice and holiness, and is the nurse of his age and the companion of his journey; —hope which is mightiest to sway the restless soul of man."

This is a basic point of all rational moralism. From the Christian standpoint it is not the only ground of hope, as we have seen. The grace and mercy of God are to be added. Yet it is essential, and it is presented by Eliphaz in one of the most forceful couplets of the poem when he says to Job in his first and most sympathetic speech:

> Is not your fear of God your confidence,
> and the integrity of your ways your hope? (4:6)

Job's Integrity

The terrible series of calamities deprive Job of everything but his life and his moral integrity, and the latter is the one supreme value which cannot be taken away from him. Moral self-confidence is the highest personal achievement of the human spirit, and it is an intrinsic value which no calamity can rob one of who has it. There is no final defeat except the inner sense of defeat; one who has conquered there has conquered everywhere. The real battle is not with the roving bands of Sabean and Chaldean marauders nor with the elements which tear down houses and barns, but with the inner man. The first to crack up on the ash heap experiences of life is the man who has a nagging and accusing conscience.

This is the second important pragmatic suggestion of the Book of Job for facing the evil of existence, after we have explored the hope beyond death. Man's first concern, for that matter, must be for his moral integrity. Practical moral experience is more important than speculations about the goodness of God or the causes of evil in the universe. Biblical religion does not permit the believer to throw all responsibility upon God or some foreign principle of evil. So when the three friends of Job turn the spotlight on his moral life, they are following the line of ethical religion. Job must face the scrutiny. He must examine himself.

The very integrity of Job makes his theoretical problem more acute. It is a strange providence which reduces all worldly ambitions of a faithful man to ashes and sores and a potsherd. But in spite of the theological mystery, his moral integrity is a practical value which keeps him unwhipped and struggling. If he had been convicted of guilt by the accusing world, he would have given up and there would have been no poem, for there would have been no problem. And his integrity has a practical value; it is his ground of hope, for it remains his one link with his Maker. Though he never comes to a theoretical solution of the mystery, he rises by a series of steps and the provocation of his friends to a positive conclusion, a final triumphant climax to his testimony. He concludes with Bildad that God will not cast away an upright man (8:20), but he applies it to himself in a different way than the insinuation of his friend. God has not entirely cast him off. Even though he be slain, he will nevertheless maintain his ways before God, knowing that if a godless man shall not come before him (13:15-16), surely a righteous man can get a hearing. Then the final series of speeches assigned to Job are a determined explication of his feeling of integrity:

> As God lives, who has taken away my right,
>   and the Almighty, who has made my soul bitter;
> as long as my breath is in me,
>   and the spirit of God is in my nostrils;
> my lips will not speak falsehood,
>   and my tongue will not utter deceit.
> Far be it from me to say that you are right;
>   till I die I will not put away my integrity from me.
> I hold fast my righteousness,
>   and will not let it go;   (27:2-6)
>   my heart does not reproach me for any of my days.

After he has reviewed his life's moral achievements and answered the charges against him with a series of disclaimers in the form of a curse, his final signature is an eloquent declaration that he will wear the indictment as a badge when he goes before the final judge:

> Oh, that I had one to hear me!
>   (Here is my signature! let the Almighty answer me!)
>   Oh, that I had the indictment written by my adversary!
> Surely I would carry it on my shoulder;
>   I would bind it on me as a crown;
> I would give him an account of all my steps;
>   like a prince I would approach him. (31:35-37)[2]

2 Most commentators take these verses to be the final word of Job, and verses 38-40 to be out of place. They fit into the pattern of the formal oaths in the earlier part of the chapter. See Edward D. Kissane, *The Book of Job* (New York: Sheed & Ward, 1946), pp. 202, 208.

The Nature of Sin

The problem of moral evil and suffering, however, cannot be solved so easily as taking a series of oaths affirming one's goodness. In a sense he is driven to that by the invectives hurled against him and the lack of insight on the part of his friends; yet his very protest yields the anxiety and uncertainty which is the common experience of men. A deeper probe into the ethical ideas of the book is needed.

Dr. Paul Weiss finds ten different kinds of evil distinguished in the Book of Job: sin, bad intention, wickedness, guilt, vice, physical suffering, psychological suffering, social suffering, natural evil, and metaphysical evil.[3] We shall adopt a simpler classification, but certain distinctions are essential. Under the head of natural evils we have already considered the suffering caused by external forces. Then we shall separate sins from moral evils. This distinction is very important and not often made. There is great ambiguity in the use of the word *sin* in all the literature from Biblical times down to the present. If the poets had made this distinction in the speeches of Eliphaz, Bildad, and Zophar, there would have been some clarification of the problem of the book. Job himself is brought in numerous verses to the verge of confession of sin (10:6, 14-15; 13:23-26; 14:16-17; 19:4), but as the argument waxes hot, the friends translate their vague insinuations into specific charges of moral evil, and Job in his defense declares his innocence and rests on his integrity. The confusion comes at this point: if one is not guilty of specific moral evils, then are we to say he cannot be judged a sinner? This is a confusion which inheres in the discussions of sin and the moral problem down to current modern literature.

Sin is always a condition of the heart of man—an attitude or inner act of thought or consent of the will which alienates the soul from God. It is internal and subjective. It can be

[3] "God, Job, and Evil," *Commentary* (August, 1948).

apprehended only by the individual who examines his own heart. Properly speaking, no person should ever be condemned by another as a sinner because the sin is not open to objective inspection. And there is no need of it because the conviction of sin is certain just the moment any person is brought to earnest introspection.

If there is no God consciousness, there is no sense of sin; but that is a situation which probably never exists so long as man is free and contemplates the meaning of his freedom. Man lives in two worlds, the world of determined things and the world of moral responsibility. All men since Adam live in relation to God so soon as they realize who their Maker is and acquire some sense of the obligations he lays upon them.

Moral evils, on the other hand, are the acts of men which are open to objective inspection and evaluation. The constant moral obligation of man is to criticize his own behavior and the activities of his society, and to work out precise methods of objective evaluation of them. The task of the moralist and the preacher is to assist in such objective evaluations. It may be assumed that evil acts are a result of the sinful condition of the soul, and that the chief way to moral living and the good society is to purify the heart. But still the distinction must be made, for it is always possible that the "good man," in terms of behavior above reproach, has not solved the problem of sin in his heart.

The Roman Catholic separation between mortal sins and venial sins is instructive in this matter. St. Thomas Aquinas defines a mortal sin as any turning of the soul away from God as its proper end. Venial sins are the disordered state of the soul without turning away from God. This distinction cannot be determined by scrutiny of the acts of men. Any immoral act may imply either mortal or venial sin.[4] Protestants consider the distinction artificial on the ground that venial sins are immoral acts which are traceable to a sinful turning

[4] *Summa Theologiae*, I, Q. 72, Art. 5.

away from God. The seven deadly sins of the Christian tradition, pride, gluttony, lust, covetousness, sloth, envy, and anger, are all words which describe primarily a condition of the heart.

In searching for the ethical ideas of the Book of Job, our first attention should be, however, to the virtues. Piety and morality belong together. That is evident in the introductory paragraph where Job is described as the upright and complete man and his piety is specified as a part of it. Truthfulness is a basic virtue, perhaps the most basic of all. Job will not practice deceit (6:28; 27:4; 31:5). He will not falsify the facts even to justify the Almighty, and the one charge of evil which he levels against the protagonists in the debate is that they are forgers of lies to support their theory of divine justice (13:4). Otherwise, the virtues extolled in the poem are justice in dealing with all people, even slaves, charity, and hospitality (29:12-17; 31:16-22, 31-32). By inference, the virtues of humility and patience are taught.

The Patience of Job

Patience is not mentioned in the book, but Job has been taken as the paragon of that virtue throughout history, and so the matter calls for scrutiny. Job was patient and yet he was not patient. He learned the importance of it the hard way, and his difficulty shows the necessity of it.

Impatience, in a sense, is a virtue in the morally sensitive man, impatience with evil and misunderstanding and the unjust lot of man. Job's impatience under the provocation of his self-righteous inquisitors is a normal reaction of man under stress, and few will fail to sympathize with him. Yet impatience is self-destructive. In the face of the evil of existence and the helplessness of man, patience is necessary to mental balance. The development of the virtue is one of the demands of the spirit in the struggle for survival.

Patience comes from a firm faith in God. So long as Job could say, "The LORD gave, and the LORD has taken away; blessed be the name of the LORD," he was a patient man. When his faith began to waver in the long dark night of the soul, he lost his patience. It was not restored until the light began to shine through the terror of the whirlwind.

The Stoics and Buddhists developed the virtue of patience as the basic principle of their ethics. In both cases it was grounded upon a faith in the rationality and the moral order of the universe. But in each case it also implies a kind of resignation to evils which is alien to the Biblical point of view. The Jew or the Christian, like Job, is patient and yet he is not patient. His rebellion against the injustices and evils of life is constant, and yet he lays down the sword at the end of the day of battle to say his prayer in patient trust in the providence of God, who alone decides the outcome.

Moral Evils

The moral evils listed in the book are more numerous than the virtues, but they also give important clues concerning the moral ideals of the time. Most of them are stated in the indictment against Job (22:1-11), or in his complaint against the prosperity of the wicked (24) and his defense (29; 31). The unbridled tongue and harsh words against fate are listed as iniquity (15:5, 13; 20:12-14). Fatness in a lean world is a mark of the wicked (15:27). Bribery (15:34), adultery (24:15; 31:9-12), thievery (24:2-4), and murder (24:14) are in the list. The thievery mentioned is not common stealing but a form of swindling by which the rich and powerful dispossess the weak of their domestic animals, the ass, the ox, and the sheep, and a form of such swindling seldom heard of in modern well-governed countries, the removal of landmarks.

The Job poets join the Hebrew prophets in their unparal-
leled protest against horrible conditions of poverty and
slavery. No words of the prophets are more vivid in condemnation of the lot of the poor or castigation of the oppressors.

> Behold, like wild asses in the desert
>   they go forth to their toil,
>   seeking prey in the wilderness
>   as food for their children.
> They gather their fodder in the field
>   and they glean the vineyard of the wicked man.
> They lie all night naked, without clothing,
>   and have no covering in the cold.
> They are wet with the rain of the mountains,
>   and cling to the rock for want of shelter.
> (There are those who snatch the fatherless child from the breast,
>   and take in pledge the infant of the poor.)
> They go about naked, without clothing;
>   hungry, they carry the sheaves;
> among the olive rows of the wicked they make oil;
>   they tread the wine presses, but suffer thirst.
> From out of the city the dying groan,
>   and the soul of the wounded cries for help;
>   yet God pays no attention to their prayer. (24:5-12)

There is no good reason to take this as a description of the
deeds of a small class of wicked oppressors. We learn from
the records of ancient India, Egypt, and Greece that everywhere in the Orient and the Occident the lot of the masses
of the people was wretched beyond description. Nowhere in
ancient literature, except in Job and the prophetic books of
the Bible, is there a protest. Even the classical moralists, like
Plato and Aristotle, accepted poverty and slavery as belong-
ing to the natural order of things.[5]

In the spirit of this protest we find further a condemnation
of anyone who takes advantage of the weak or who exploits

[5] On these conditions and the importance of the protest of Job, see Moses
Buttenwieser, *The Book of Job* (New York: The Macmillan Co., 1925),
pp. 254 ff.

need and poverty (22:6; 31:21-22). Oppression and violence
are evils (20:19; 27:13-19), as also a lack of charity toward
the needy (22:7, 19; 24:7; 26:2) and a failure to deal fairly
with slaves (31:13-15). A bad use of the land is deplored
(31:38), and this passage might be linked with another in
which soil erosion is recognized as one of the natural evils
(14:19).

Sins

All moral evils stem from sinfulness in the heart. Sin is
not mere feeling. Anxiety and guilt are feelings but not sins.
They are the condition and the confirmation of sin. Sin is an
act, too; an internal act, a thought, an intent, an attitude, in
which the free will turns away from God. This inwardness
of the source of evil comes to more profound recognition in
the Book of Job than in any other part of the Old Testament.
"Does Job fear God for nought?" implies that insincerity and
self-interest lie in the heart of the best of men. Just as truthfulness is the basic virtue, so deceitfulness is a basic sin and
lying a grievous moral evil (13:4; 15:35; 31:5). Lying is always a sign of insecurity, modern psychologists say, and that
is the same thing as a lack of faith. Lying is the evil act which
has deceit and faithlessness as its sinful background. Other
specific sins recognized in the book are covetousness (31:7),
trust in riches (31:24-25), and lust (31:1, 9). In the Law and
the prophets, acts of adultery and vengeance are sins, but Job
takes a position similar to that of Jesus who said that one who
looks on a woman in lust has committed adultery already in
his heart, and to hate a brother is to be guilty of murder. For
Job it is sin even to desire retaliation or to take inward pleasure
at the suffering of one's enemies (31:29-30).

The chief import of the Book of Job, however, is its bear-
ing on the sin of pride and the virtue of humility. In the
Christian analysis of the moral life since the works of St.
Augustine, sins are distinguished as those which grow out of

pride and those which belong to sensuality. Pride is man's innate resistance to the acceptance of the lot of a creature, wholly dependent on God, and his tendency to usurp the functions of deity. Sensuality is the moving of the spirit to escape from the anxieties which attend upon freedom and responsibility into an excessive indulgence of the appetites. These have their end and good as they sustain life, not as they provide pleasure as an end in itself.[6]

Pride

The meaning of pride as sin takes its first historical definition from Greek tragic literature. The tragic hero, such as Prometheus and Oedipus, was guilty of what was called *hubris*. This is usually translated *insolence*, but it contains the basic element which the Christians have called *pride*. The hero is a superman who plunges blindly into a program in which his own will and sense of rightness is placed above submission to the gods. This is insolence to the gods for which the hero must suffer, but it is both the doing and the suffering which makes him the tragic hero. The situation is paradoxical because he is guilty and yet it is fated that he should be guilty.

The tragic hero kind of *hubris* does not appear in the Bible. Even Job is not a tragic hero, for his involvement in suffering is not the work of his own aggressive and violent will; it is the work of demonic forces in nature, and Job is never guilty of the swaggering violence of the superman. But the pride of man which is the basic self-exaltation element in the Greek *hubris* appears many times. It is the sin of nations, according to the prophets. Rulers exalt themselves to heaven and shall be brought low. That classic passage in Isaiah which speaks of the fall of Lucifer, the day star is a case in point. A Babylonian king is in the prophet's thought.

[6] Following Reinhold Niebuhr's treatment in *The Nature and Destiny of Man* (New York: Chas. Scribner's Sons, 1946), Vol. I, Chap. vii.

How you are fallen from heaven,
  O Day Star, son of Dawn!
How you are cut down to the ground,
  you who laid the nations low!
You said in your heart,
  "I will ascend to heaven;
above the stars of God
  I will set my throne on high;
I will sit on the mount of assembly
  in the far north;
I will ascend above the heights of the clouds,
  I will make myself like the Most High."
But you are brought down to Sheol,
  to the depths of the Pit. (Isa. 14:12-15)

Pride goeth before the fall of nations (Prov. 16). When Lucifer came to be identified with Satan, then pride was established as the basic sin of Satan himself, the cause of the primeval fall from heaven, and the origin of all sin in man because it is the very act of turning away from God as man's proper end.

The source of all sinfulness in Biblical thought, in both Old and New Testaments, is perhaps better described as lack of faith, and the most dramatic form which this takes is idolatry. Man must have no other gods, but always he is tempted to turn the creatures of proximity, in their mystery and man's fearfulness of them, into objects of worship. There is just an echo of this in the Book of Job:

if I have looked at the sun when it shone,
  or the moon moving in splendor,
and my heart has been secretly enticed,
  and my mouth has kissed my hand;
this also would be an iniquity to be punished by the judges,
  for I should have been false to God above. (31:26-28)

Among the Jews such idolatry played a large part, and in a broader sense it does among us, for it is simply that prideful spirit by which man always exalts himself and his creatures. It is required of the religious man that he recognize his creatureliness and its limitations at the same time that he turns his heart toward God.

> All flesh is grass,
>> and all its beauty is like the flower of the field.
>
> *   *   *   *   *
>
> The grass withers, the flower fades;
>> but the word of our God will stand for ever.
>>> (Isa. 40:6, 8)

Job recognized such creatureliness,

> Man that is born of a woman
>> is of few days, and full of trouble.
> He comes forth like a flower, and withers;
>> he flees like a shadow, and continues not. (14:1-2)

But he had difficulty in grasping that word of God which shall stand forever.

Was Job Guilty of Pride?

The friends start their abortive efforts at consoling Job by insinuating that he lacks wisdom, and they dispense it to him in the form of the orthodox notion of divine justice. Job's response opens a contest as to which has the track of wisdom (11:5-6; 12:2-3). Whoever wrote and inserted the twenty-eighth chapter into the document had an insight about wisdom which both parties needed to learn:

> Whence then comes wisdom?
>> And where is the place of understanding?
> It is hid from the eyes of all living,
>> and concealed from the birds of the air.
>
> *   *   *   *   *
>
> God understands the way to it,
>> and he knows its place.
>
> *   *   *   *   *
>
> And he said to man,
> "Behold, the fear of the LORD, that is wisdom;
>> and to depart from evil is understanding."
>>> (28:20-21, 23, 28)

This would seem to say that a sinful pride is inevitable to any human pretense of wisdom. Job's stout assertion of his integrity brings from the friends the more direct accusation that he is guilty of boasting and impiety, which amounts to the same thing. Whenever anyone falls into the claim that

> . . . My doctrine is pure,
> and I am clean in God's eyes. (11:4)

then the net result is bound to be,

> But you are doing away with the fear of God,
> and hindering meditation before God. (15:4)

Zophar and Eliphaz lay hold upon a fundamental truth there, whatever judgment we may pass upon their unkindliness in the attack.

Job is not convicted of the kind of self-interest which Satan's sneer implies. His piety and morality are not a calculated bid for the prosperity which came to him. But consider what happens to a man who does live a good life and prospers by it and then suddenly comes on this sort of crisis. It is very difficult for a rich man to get into the kingdom of heaven; next to impossible, according to Jesus. This is because his success is certain to be a proof to him that he is virtuous. How can he escape sinful pride? Then, in the crisis, he is offended by insinuations of his own involvement in guilt. His resentment is certain to take the form of blame upon others, his neighbors, or fate, or God himself under a system of religious doctrine like that of ancient Judaea. And one does not need to be rich to fall into this predicament; all that is needed is a situation where some project of the good life is frustrated. "Pride is the inordinate appetite of excellence," says St. Thomas Aquinas, and it is at the point of crisis in pursuit of excellence that pride exhibits itself as resentment toward others or toward God.

When the friends go on to list a catalogue of specific evils against Job (22:5-11), the debate has degenerated into stiff-

necked stubbornness. They are too deeply involved in the
same sort of worldly pride to be able to see Job's situation
clearly. Job categorically denies the wickedness and goes on
to castigate evils which they had not thought of. None of the
specific charges are pinned on him. He holds fast his integrity
to the last triumphant shout of the debate. There is a certain
glory in this unwhipped sense of integrity while he faces the
superficial criticisms of his friends, yet the very assertion of
his strength leads him into the sin of pride. This is the trap
set for every good man.

Dread

With all his protests of innocence, there breathes throughout the speeches of Job a profound anxiety. It comes to its
most poignant expression in 9:28-31:

> I become afraid of all my suffering,
>> for I know thou wilt not hold me innocent.
> I shall be condemned;
>> why then do I labor in vain?
> If I wash myself with snow,
>> and cleanse my hands with lye,
> yet thou wilt plunge me into a pit,
>> and my own clothes will abhor me.

Proud man in his most confident assertions of integrity is
caught in the sense of dread, to use an expression which the
translators of Kierkegaard have made current for this feeling.
The Danish theologian makes a startling distinction between
dread as experienced in the pagan character and dread in the
Jewish experience. Pagan dread stands in relation to fate,
which he defines as the unity of necessity and chance. But
the Jewish experience of dread is related to guilt. In the Biblical world, the sense of freedom and moral responsibility are
more acute. In its deepest sense, says Kierkegaard, the concept of guilt and sin does not emerge in paganism.[7] This dis-

[7] Sören A. Kierkegaard, *The Concept of Dread* (Princeton: Princeton
University Press, 1946), pp. 86-98.

tinction illuminates the characteristic difference between Job and the Greek tragic hero. For example, compare the above words of Job with the following passage from Prometheus, the suffering Titan, bound to the cliff in punishment for his defiance of Zeus:

> Woes that are here, and woes that are to come
> Afflict my spirit. Vast, unending gloom!
> What light shall bring a limit to my doom?
> What am I saying? All is known to me,
> All, all that is to be;—nor with fresh smart
> Shall one pang smite me. Then let me endure
> My destiny as I may, knowing that none
> May e'er bid battle to Necessity.[8]

The tragic hero solves his problem of dread by courage in the face of fate. He does not repent; he acknowledges no guilt. The Jew or Christian must annul his dread by repentance and faith. Dread of guilt is not the same thing as guilt, as dread is not sin. It is rather the nurturing soil of sin and guilt, and until it is resolved by faith, as it had not yet been in the case of Job, then sin and guilt are inevitable. For every spirit nurtured in the Biblical thought and faith, this dread is the quality which lends to every assertion of certainty a feeling of uncertainty and to every protestation of innocence a feeling of guilt.

It must be recognized that there are two uses of the word *guilt* in our tradition. It is the difference between Augustine and Pelagius. The Pelagians are the strict rational moralists who connect guilt only with moral responsibility. Many of these would say that man is guilty only when he is fully aware of having committed an evil deed. On this view, if Job had not broken the law nor committed any of the acts of moral evil charged against him, then he could not be guilty. But the Book of Job itself and the tragic sort of guilt which be-

[8] Aeschylus *Prometheus Bound*, translated by Lewis Campbell in The World's Classics (New York: Oxford University Press, 1906), lines 99-106.

longs to the Greek tradition and Augustine's struggle with the nature of original sin, against Pelagius, are all more profound in their insight into human nature. Such is the depth and power of man's sensuousness and his will to power that he suffers from guilt feelings even when his impulses are under nearly perfect control. If, as Paul Tillich has said, "We experience freedom as responsibility, and destiny as tragic," [9] then guilt involves more than awareness of responsibility; we are involved in tragic guilt.

The Final Issue of the Drama

While we may depreciate the poetic quality of the Elihu speeches and judge them to be the work of a later hand, yet their author senses a lack in the symposium. Only once does the word pride appear, and that in a doubtful verse (33:17), but the burden of Elihu's message is just that. And he directs the charge not only against Job but against the three friends as well. They are equally guilty and their blindness on this point renders their defense of orthodoxy inadequate.

> For has any one said to God,
>   "I have borne chastisement; I will not offend any more;
> teach me what I do not see;
>   if I have done iniquity, I will do it no more"?
>
> *   *   *   *   *
>
> "Job speaks without knowledge,
>   his words are without insight.
> Would that Job were tried to the end,
>   because he answers like wicked men.
> For he adds rebellion to his sin;
>   he claps his hands among us,
>   and multiplies his words against God." (34:31-32, 35-37)

The voice from the whirlwind gives proud man a dose of mystery and majesty designed to awe and humble him. The

[9] From a lecture given at the Union Theological Seminary, New York City. But see his discussion of freedom and destiny in his *Systematic Theology* (Chicago: University of Chicago Press, 1951), Vol. I, pp. 182 ff.

speeches of Yahweh are an enigma to all efforts at rational interpretation. Some find in them only "an impotent collapse" before an absoluteness which modern philosophers seek in one way or another to reject.[10] But there is something here more profound than impotent collapse. There is humbleness, confession, and restoration—spiritual restoration, even though one may regard the reported rewards of new flocks and children as artificial and spurious.

The epilogue has always been a puzzle to interpreters. Why should the LORD condemn Eliphaz and his two friends so roundly for declaring the very orthodox theory of retribution which is confirmed by the events related in the passage? They are bidden to make sacrifices, and Job is commended and asked to pray for them (42:7-9).

The best answer seems to be that Job had been humbled and they had not been. In fact, they had been most guilty all the way through of the sins of pride. Why is it that as we follow their speeches we dislike them all intensely? It is not because we disagree radically with the burden of their argument. Their words are truly words of wisdom, more quoted in the text of religious education than the words of Job. And it is not entirely our sympathy with the suffering one. Isn't it just that feeling of pride with which the comfortable one points the finger of scorn at the sufferer? His affluence he takes to be a special mark of divine favor and confirmation of his own goodness. It is pride, not expressed in words of boasting, but in attitude. And this sort of pride is always instinctively detected and despised among men.

Job is brought to humble repentance; but the friends need it more than he. Obedience to ritual demands for sacrifices may accomplish it but it seldom does. Usually it takes suffer-

<hr />

[10] In a letter, Edgar S. Brightman has said, "the theophany from the whirlwind repels me as an *argumentum ad baculum.*" See his criticism of absolutism in his *A Philosophy of Religion* (New York: Prentice-Hall, Inc., 1940), pp. 307-13.

ing. Who can learn the lesson of Job unless he has to sit on the ash heap with him!

This is not to say, in recognizing the prideful aspect of Job's problem, that all sufferings are merited as retribution. To be without pride under such circumstances would be a kind of saintliness which men who have inherited the sin of Adam do not manifest.

And does all this mean that the cultivation of some vices might save one from the sin of pride? If pride is involved in the sense of integrity, why is the integrity so important? The question calls up the similar question which confronted St. Paul, "Are we to continue in sin that grace may abound?" (Rom. 6:1). The answer must be No! in either case. General Walter Bedell Smith in his book, My Three Years in Moscow, speaking of Molotov, says that he is "without redeeming minor vices." The inference is that the "coldly self-possessed" communist leader might be less fearsome as a prideful dictator if his rigid excellence were relieved by minor vices. That depends: if one recognizes one's vices as vices and is properly ashamed of them, they might contribute some to one's humility, but the pride of man is such that he usually thinks of his vices as virtues and wants to impose them on all around him.

Job is happily free from that worst form of the sin of pride which is that of the swaggering superman who conceives his destiny to require the liquidation of all opponents to his will and ideology. Paul Weiss finds the exposure of all forms of pride to be one of the main values of this work. He says, "If the Book of Job be any guide, we must oppose those contemporary prophets who affirm that God's wisdom is ours, and what we take to be good, God will eventually endorse." [11]

[11] See note 3, above.

Chapter 10

SUFFERING AS DISCIPLINE

St. Francis and Brother Leo

A beautiful passage in *The Little Flowers of St. Francis* dramatically portrays the religious spirit in one of its most inspiring moods. St. Francis and Brother Leo are on their way from Perugia to the mountain retreat of St. Mary of the Angels. It is a cold and rainy day. The Saint is instructing Brother Leo in the source of perfect joy as they pick their way along the path. It is not in deeds of charity and ministration, nor in the knowledge of all science and all eloquence, that perfect joy is to be found, but

> When we
> Shall to Saint Mary of the Angels come,
> Soaked thus with rain, and frozen with the cold,
> And mud-bespattered and with hunger spent,
> Knock at the House-door, and the porter comes
> In wrath, and asks: "Who are ye?" and we say:
> "Two of your Brethren we," and he replies:
> "Nay, but ye say not sooth, two rogues ye are
> Who go about cozening the world, to rob
> The poor man of his alms; away with you!"
> Nor will not open to us, and makes us stand
> Out in the rain and snow, hungry and cold,
> Even until nightfall; then, if all these wrongs,
> And all this cruelty, and these rude rebuffs,
> We shall in patience, without soreness, bear,
> And murmur not against him, and shall think
> With charity and meekness that indeed
> The porter knows us, and was moved by God
> To our abuse; O Brother Leo, write
> That herein there is perfect joy.

*   *   *   *   *

And if, with cold and hunger and the night
Sore pressed, yet knock and call we, praying him
With loud plaints, for the love of God, to ope
And let us in, and he, the more enraged,
Shall say: "Lo! these be knaves importunate;
Now will I pay them that they have deserved,"
And with a knotty staff shall issue forth,
And hale us by the hood, and fling to earth,
And roll us in the snow, and with that staff
Belabour, knot by knot—if all these things
We shall with patience joyfully endure,
Weighing the sufferings of the blessèd Christ,
The which for His love's sake we ought to bear—
Here and herein, O Brother Leo, write
Is perfect joy.[1]

The writer of the Epistle to the Hebrews set the final touch to the Christian conception of the values obtainable through suffering by saying that the most perfect man who ever lived was made perfect through suffering (2:10). This is a sentiment of moving beauty. How different the idea sounds however, when it comes from one of Job's comfortable comforters:

Behold, happy is the man whom God reproves;
   therefore despise not the chastening of the Almighty. (5:17)

There would be a different ring in the words if they were in the mouth of Job. The idea is a little more tolerable in the words of the youthful and unsophisticated Elihu:

He delivers the afflicted by their affliction,
   and opens their ear by adversity. (36:15)

The speeches of Elihu elaborate at some length the idea that suffering has a corrective and thereby very practical purpose in human experience, and when we examine the doctrine with proper qualifications we find another of those pragmatic

[1] From James Rhoades' translation in The World's Classics (New York: Oxford University Press, 1925).

suggestions by which the religious consciousness faces the evil of existence.

The value of suffering as discipline is one of the major themes of the Job drama, set first of all by the Satan episode, as we have seen in a previous discussion of that passage. Popular interpretations of the book have always found here a mysterious cause of innocent suffering. Sinners suffer as punishment for their sins, but saints must bear affliction by design of an inscrutable providence to test and strengthen the quality of their righteousness. Eliphaz (5:17-26) gives to the notion an eloquent exposition, but he is too much involved in the theory of retribution to penetrate profoundly into the matter. Elihu does that better, though with less eloquence.

And we must note that the interpretation of the LORD as a testing and disciplining deity is a prominent feature of the prophetic tradition after Jeremiah. For the weeping prophet, the LORD was a searcher of the mind and trier of the heart.

> The heart is deceitful above all things,
>   and desperately corrupt;
>   who can understand it?
> "I the LORD search the mind
>   and try the heart,
> to give to every man according to his ways,
>   according to the fruit of his doings." (Jer. 17:9-19)

One of the anonymous prophets of the Greek period sees the persecutions of the people by false shepherds as a refining fire: The LORD "will refine them as silver is refined, and will try them as gold is tried" A psalmist addresses the LORD thus:

> Search me, O God, and know my heart!
>   Try me and know my thoughts!
> And see if there be any wicked way in me,
>   (Psalms 139:23-24)

Job, also, in those words which echo another psalmist's wonder at the dignity of man, accepts the divine testing process but with a sad complaint:

> What is man, that thou dost make so much of him,
>   and that thou dost set thy mind upon him,
> dost visit him every morning,
>   and test him every moment? (7:17-18)[2]

As a theoretical explanation of the problem of evil, the testing deity must be rejected. The LORD's giving man into the hands of Satan for a trial of his piety is a notion which the Book of Job forever refutes. But to accept adversity as the occasion for introspection and self-discipline requires true humility and is a sample of the pragmatic approach of religion to life.

The Nature of Suffering

The exposition of suffering as discipline requires several important considerations on the nature of suffering.

First, suffering is a personal experience, and a person is a complex organic unity. Afflictions cannot be set apart from the total experience and treated as though they were separate entities. Just as there is no error apart from wrong thinking, and no moral evil apart from evil deeds, so there is no misery apart from the kind of functioning of the organism which leads either to physical or mental pain. Any specific case of suffering must therefore be estimated in its relation to the total situation. The athlete staggers and fairly falls across the line as he puts his last bit of strength into the finish of the long race. In an agony of gasping for breath, he lies on his blanket. The enthusiasm of the spectators never considers the pain of the runner, for the race is won. Neither does the

[2] J. M. Powis Smith, in his *The Old Testament: An American Translation* (Chicago: The University of Chicago Press, 1931), uses the word "inspect" instead of "visit" in this passage.

runner think of it. The shout of his name, the hazy chant of
the college yell in his swooning consciousness, and all is well.
But then the race may be lost. Not all suffering has such an
outcome. When unrewarded and unexplained, suffering has
a tendency to be isolated and become a problem.

Second, we must distinguish between the possibility and
the actuality of suffering. In the case of error, sin, and moral
evil, such a distinction is more obvious. The possibility of
error is necessary to the development of free intelligence, and
the possibility of sin is necessary to moral character; yet truth
involves the absence of error, and moral perfection the absence of sin.

The possibility of pain is necessary to the discipline of
habit, although the avoidance of pain is one of the main
objects of life, even though with the followers of Epicurus,
we do not take it as an ultimate good. If a child felt no pain
from scorched fingers, he would not learn to keep out of the
fire with multiplied parental scoldings; and a kind of parental
discipline which substitutes the scoldings for a normal allot-
ment of pain is hardly good education. Parents must be
aware of the difference between physical pain and mental
suffering, and when pain is inflicted as punishment they must
be very cautious with regard to mental types of anguish which
cause the child anxiety and insecurity. The spanking may not
be half so serious as the typical scolding.

The possibility of mental suffering is also necessary to
elementary self-preservation and perhaps to mature psychic
health as well. Fear is intense suffering, but it is very useful
at times. Nothing is more certain to result in physical,
mental, social, and moral disintegration than the habitual use
of narcotics for the relief of pain, especially mental pain,
whether the narcosis be from the effects of alcohol or the
extracts of the poppy. This does not mean, however, that
the realization of suffering, or the infliction of it, especially
as a protracted experience, is either a necessity or a good.

Error, sin, and tribulations, as Ralph Tyler Flewelling has pointed out, are "schoolmasters of life," but they can be such only as they remain largely potential. As soon as they become "taskmasters," they are neither teachers nor builders but destroyers.[3]

Third, it is the dramatic character of some suffering which calls our attention sharply to the evil of the world. Eighteenth-century Europe, enlightened and rationalistic, believing this to be the best of all possible worlds, was periodically visited by pestilence, was almost continuously at war, and the lot of the common toilers, everywhere bad, was gradually degraded by the Industrial Revolution and the rise of capitalism; yet it took the Lisbon earthquake in November, 1755, to call forth a flood of literary protest against the goodness of God. Within two months Voltaire had published a poem on the event, and it figured in *Candide*, the novel in which he satirized the optimistic view of providence. A wave of chiliasm swept over Europe, with predictions of the immediate end of an evil world and the beginning of the millennium.[4]

The wars of the twentieth century have released a flood of pessimism, but the comparison of the number of deaths in war and by accident is startling. According to figures widely published in 1951, the United States in that year passed the one-millionth mark in the number of deaths both in warfare and in traffic accidents. By September of that year, the total number of American military personnel killed in all wars since 1775 was one million; and in December the millionth death in the United States occurred on a highway, counting from the first recorded motor traffic death in 1899. During the first year of the Korean War there were three

[3] Ralph Tyler Flewelling, *The Reason in Faith* (New York: Abingdon-Cokesbury Press, 1924), Chap. ix.
[4] A recent study of this event by Edgar S. Brightman is "The Lisbon Earthquake: A Study in Religious Valuation," *American Journal of Theology*, Vol. 23 (1919).

times as many killed in traffic at home as lost their lives in Korea. Industrial accidents took the lives of 796,500 people in a forty-three year period from 1907 to 1950. These attract less public attention than the traffic victims. Death in an automobile or a factory is quite as costly in anguish as in battle, and the victim is much more likely to be an innocent person.

Reformers know the worth of dramatized suffering. The blood of the martyrs became the seed of the early Church. In a former age of theological tyranny, the heretic met his end in a blaze of glory with a good deal of excitement about it. In an age which has given up the belief in fiery punishments, methods of torture are less dramatic and more effective. Modern revolutionary leaders like to make martyrs out of others for propaganda purposes; there is no hurry to take that role for themselves. Communists rush to the defense of every Negro caught in the meshes of the law, not to defend the prisoner from injustice but to create a case exhibit of the racial discrimination of bourgeois society.

If suffering is to have a proper pragmatic value, we must have a deeper concern for it in all its forms than the comfortable and nonchalant citizen who shrugs his shoulders at poverty and quotes Abraham Lincoln, "God must have loved the poor, for he made so many of them"; and we must treat it in a more intelligent fashion than the noblewoman who wept copiously over the dramatic sufferings of the hero in the opera while her coachman froze to death in the bitter storm outside.

Fourth, suffering is real in all its forms. Break an arm or fall into a delirious fever, and the agony is no illusion. Sorrows for the sins of a wayward child or remorse at failure as a parent, is genuine anguish. When Job scraped his boils with the potsherd, the pain was no delusion. When Jesus the Christ bore the lash and was nailed to the cross, his agony was real. One may be able to convince one's self that it is all for the best; that good is bound to come out of it; but by no stretch of the imagination can the reality of the pain be denied. The denial of suffering has a ludicrous analogy in the dentist, back in times when anesthetics were new, who advertised himself as a painless practitioner. In the course of an extraction, a patient gave a loud yell. "Now see here, you mustn't do that. Don't you know I am a painless dentist?" With proper indignation the patient replied, "Well, you may be painless, but I'm not." There is no practical solution of the problem by identifying either physical or mental pain with error or illusion.

Fifth, physical pain is not the worst form of suffering. Mental and spiritual aspects are more intense. Job's severest trial came not from the first Satanic impact, the loss of goods, children, and even the attack upon his skin; it was the spiritual struggle which resulted: the sense of estrangement from God, the loss of early faith, and feelings of despair and remorse.[5]

One who conquers the mental aspect of his suffering ordinarily finds the physical aspects readily surmountable. The Job story shows the necessity of a spiritual work in healing. (The chief agony of Jesus took place in Gethsemane, and when he had been assured of the heavenly Father's will he was prepared for the ordeal of the cross.) William McDougall illustrates the possibility of mental control over pain by the story of Archbishop Cranmer in the flames at Oxford. From his prison tower he watched his two friends, Latimer and Ridley, burn in the square below. Master Ridley was weak and cringing but Latimer encouraged him with the famous words that they were lighting a candle in England that should

[5] Traces of remorse are hard to find in the words of Job, although 10:14-15 and 13:23-24 imply guilt and remorse to a degree. The strength of the assertion of integrity would suppress its opposite, remorse. This is perhaps the single way in which the work deals abstractly with a problem. It is psychologically improbable that in a similar situation there would be no feeling of remorse.

never be put out. Cranmer weakened under the strain and signed a humiliating recantation. Then, regaining his courage before the ecclesiastical court, he withdrew the document, and when he stood at the stake he held the offending right hand in the flames until it burned to a stump, and spoke comforting words to the bystanders. The sense of inner victory, the absence of fear, and complete resignation, reinforced by counter emotions of remorse and hate, make such a thing possible.[6]

Suffering and Retribution

Any device which can relieve the mind of its fear and anxiety is good for the relief of more than half of all suffering. The minister is as important as the physician in illness, and the doctor's counseling and bedside manner are an important part of his practice. This fact is the strength of the faith-healing cults. Orthodox Christianity is in possession of all the elements of an adequate faith, but religious thought still needs to be divested of some fear-breeding beliefs carried over from prescientific stages of human thought. One of these is the belief held by Job's friends that all suffering is direct punishment for sin. More serious than the belief itself is the set of attitudes so often generated by it. The doctrine of retribution, as it is called, belongs to the concise and circumscribed world view of former times, and it has deeply affected the theological notions that were formulated under that scheme, although there has always been a protest against it, such as we have in the Book of Job.

Herbert Wildon Carr presented an important exposition of the way the doctrine has tended to add to the burden of human woe by increasing anxiety, and also the direction in

[6] William McDougall, *Outline of Psychology* (New York: Chas. Scribner's Sons, 1929), p. 268. There are variations in this story, and his account has been compared with that of G. P. Fisher, *History of the Christian Church* (New York: Chas. Scribner's Sons, 1914), pp. 360-61.

which the modern scientific approach to such problems tends to modify the doctrine.[7] For illustration, he calls attention to the traditional attitude toward the suffering of women in childbirth. It is the most mysterious case of pain in the whole realm of experience. Parturition is a perfectly normal life process, and ordinarily the normal processes are accompanied by pleasure. Pain is usually the signal of some unnatural or harmful process. The mystery of it has marked womanhood with the brand of degradation in practically every ancient culture, and in many of them the pain has been interpreted as punitive. Early Christians explained the mystery by attaching it to the sin of Eve, and the Pastoral Epistle of Timothy absolves Adam, laying the chief responsibility on Eve. Childbirth pains are the evidence of it and price of woman's redemption (I Tim. 2:14-15).

The whole pathetic history of the lot of woman has been involved in such doctrines as this. Man's bondage to a theory has laid upon them, in addition to the natural suffering, the mental stigma of moral inferiority and spiritual pollution. All religions, including Christianity, have required ceremonial cleansings which have enslaved women everywhere to vile superstitions before the coming of the scientific enlightenment. It can hardly be said that science has cleared away all the mystery of pain, but to this case it can assign a rational answer. The pain serves a useful biological function: occurring at the proper moment, it secures the physical response needed for a safe and rapid delivery. The pain thus serves a racial purpose which disregards the individual's demand for pleasure as the mark of all goodness.

The hedonistic theory of the good has always exercised an undue influence upon the development of theological

[7] H. W. Carr, *Changing Backgrounds of Religion and Ethics* (New York: The Macmillan Co., 1927), Chap. xi. This work makes the mistake of taking the retributive theory as regulative for all Christian doctrines in their historical development. It misses the paradoxical aspect of the doctrine of the atonement.

doctrine, in spite of the fact that nearly all religious teachers have warned against the pursuit of pleasure as an end in life. This is an aspect of the equivocal situation which confronts a practical approach to these problems. Pleasure is a value, and yet all pain cannot be taken as an evil or the sign of some hidden punishment for evil. Much suffering is the direct result of moral evil, but not all. To quarrel with the retributive theory is not to imply that suffering is never punitive. The major premise of the religious interpretation of experience may be said to be the proposition that *all sin leads to suffering*. The conclusion of the retributive theory is that *all suffering is a result of sin*. But this is an invalid conversion of the first premise. It can be converted logically only by reduction, *some suffering is the result of sin*.

Another indication of double meaning in the situation cannot be pointed out too often. So long as the sufferer takes his suffering as an occasion for self-examination, there may be some merit in the idea; but when the notion of retribution becomes a standard by which one interprets another's suffering, it is the occasion for some very unlovely social experience.

Modern science has introduced an important and complicated distinction into our thinking by calling certain evils *disease*. A disease is a special area of human suffering which can be isolated for study by the objective methods of science. Most of the diseases have in past times been looked upon primarily as moral problems, and the theological and purposive interpretation of suffering as punishment for sin has acted too often as a deterrent to scientific progress. That is the chief reason that scientists have often been hostile to theology and teleological metaphysics.

To call a type of suffering, such as tuberculosis or alcoholism, a disease is not to say that it is in no way concerned with sin or moral evil, but it surrounds the problem with an attitude that differs from mere social disapproval. It searches for causes and routines of cure and prevention. And it has the value of relieving the mind of the sufferer from a burden of social condemnation, no matter how much he may need to square his spiritual relation with his God. No one is more ready to recognize the need of a spiritual approach to the same problems, and the inadequacy of pure physiology, than modern well-schooled medical practitioners.

Pain an Instrumental Value

All physical pain can be assigned a biological function. Pain is a specific sensation, like touch or taste or sight. This is a discovery of recent times. In the corium of the skin all over the body, and in the mucous linings inside the body, there are terminal nerve end organs which give a sense of pain when stimulated. Students in the psychological laboratory locate some of these organs with a pointed instrument and chart their location on the skin. They are interspersed in varying densities with the heat and cold and pressure organs. Physical pain, therefore, must be distinguished from mental displeasure, and it is not a true opposite of pleasure. It is a sensation, while both pleasure and displeasure are emotions. This means that pain is not simply a disvalue but a positive instrumental value. Not all displeasure is disvaluable either, for it may have an instrumental value as a stimulus to something better. Pain, pleasure, displeasure, all must be evaluated by criteria which go beyond the experiences themselves to see the "happiness" or "rightness" of the organism as a whole.

The instrumental value of pain and displeasure may be stated as discipline, and it is necessary for the elementary tasks of life. The most obvious illustrations could be drawn from the training of children; but in a sense we are all children: we do not learn to keep out of the fire until we get our fingers burnt.

The children of Job were having a drinking party in the eldest son's home when the tornado hit. Job's solicitude for his sons appeared in his daily devotions. Bildad insinuates that there was an involvement of sin on the part of the children (8:4). While there is no implication that wine was a factor in the charge, and to say that the tornado was a direct punishment from divine providence is absurd on the face of it; yet a rich man's discipline for his sons is always a problem. What father is without anxiety on the matter? Koheleth's cynicism about the vanity of riches might have had some connection with the spectacle of David and Absalom: "Then I considered all that my hands had done and the toil I had spent in doing it, and behold, all was vanity and a striving after wind, and there was nothing to be gained under the sun" (Eccles. 2:11). When sons are spared the pain which is instrumental and disciplinary, it is likely before long that they will run into the pain which is punitive.

St. Augustine, writing in *The City of God* to the pagan society of the Roman Empire in its day of trial, tells the Romans that they are the victims of the double evil of those whose wickedness brings suffering upon them and whose blindness causes them to miss the lesson. "Depraved by good fortune, and not chastened by adversity, what you desire in the restoration of a peaceful and secure state, is not the tranquillity of the commonwealth, but the impunity of your own vicious luxury." [8] What a message this is for the people of modern society who are more concerned about their living standard than about the justice and security of the world!

Pain as discipline needs no extended demonstration, but is that the ultimate reason for suffering? If suffering is nothing but discipline, then the blood drawn by the lash on the back of the slave is simply to teach him to hoe his row; the lynching of a few black men is a divinely appointed means of doing what some white men have claimed for it: showing

[8] *The City of God*, I, 33.

the Negro how to keep his place; the cursing and cruelty of some army officers is good for discipline; the privations and hard knocks of the laboring man are to break his spirit, and make him content with his lot and learn the folly of ambition.

The prize fighter abuses himself and hires other men to beat him that he may be able to stand punishment. That is discipline, and the doctrine that all suffering is disciplinary is on the prize-fight level of values. So long as one takes the hard knocks which come to him as discipline for himself, and steels his muscles and his character to withstand the world, suffering has value as such. There is even a certain beauty in the attitude when we see it in a saint like Francis of Assisi. But just so soon as anyone makes this theory an excuse for his hardness toward the sufferings of others, or a justification of the vast suffering which is caused by man's inhumanity to man, then the doctrine becomes positively vicious.

Suffering and Human Progress

Plato, in the tenth book of the *Republic*, passes a severe judgment upon the poet: "He is a manufacturer of images and is very far removed from the truth." The tragic poets in particular, he says, educate the passions rather than inform the reason. They imitate the worst evils and sufferings of men, and the crowd of the theater is enthralled by the hero's impassioned speeches about his woes which would be a shameful performance for any man off the stage. If poets are permitted in the ideal republic, then it will not be law and reason but pleasure and pain that will rule the state. What Plato proposes as the proper approach to evil breathes a modern practical spirit. He says

> That we should take counsel about what has happened, and when the dice have been thrown order our affairs in the way which reason deems best; not, like children who have had a fall, keeping hold of the part struck and wasting time in setting up

a howl, but always accustoming the soul forthwith to apply a remedy, raising up that which is sickly and fallen, banishing the cry of sorrow by the healing art.[9]

Few today would be so severe as Plato, but he has a point with interesting application to the Job poem. Perhaps the stage setting of the Job story bears some resemblance to the performance of ancient desert people in the land of Uz when confronted with dire suffering. Since the hand of God was against the victim, he was banished to the ash dump and his friends approached with extreme and superstitious caution. How much different the modern pragmatic attack upon the problem would be!

In a situation like that of Job today, friends would not come around and sit seven days in silence and then carry on a protracted argument about the meaning of it all. They would call an ambulance and hurry the victim off to a hospital where his disease would not only be subjected to curative treatment with miracle drugs, radiation, and dietary regulation, including vitamins, but it would also be the subject of scientific research in the interest of preventing its recurrence in others. A collection would be taken to purchase several young ewes and a blooded ram, and the neighbors would take turns tending the new flock while Job is in the hospital. A vigilance committee would deal with the Sabeans and Chaldeans in the future. When it is all over they might sit around on Sunday afternoon and reflect on the meaning of it all.

Modern enlightened society has caught to some extent the spirit of Jesus in the story of the Good Samaritan. The priest and the Levite went by on the other side of the road away from the dying victim of the robbers, not because they were vicious at heart nor just because they had on the spotless robes of their office. They had a neat intellectual explanation for all such tragedies which absolved them from any respon-

[9] Plato, *Republic*, X, 604. (Jowett translation.)

sibility. The Good Samaritan ministered to the man without asking any questions other than the extent of his need.

All evil is a challenge to men. Good is always an achievement which involves subordination of evil. The greatest heroes are those who have taken some great evil as a challenge to sacrificial leadership: Lincoln battling for liberation and unity, Livingstone toiling to open a dark continent to light and progress. The optimism of Robert Browning was based upon a clear apprehension that progress lies through suffering and struggle with evils, not, as sometimes assumed, in a blindness for the evils themselves. In *A Death in the Desert*, the poet says that man

> . . . in this striving, this converting air
> Into a solid he may grasp and use,
> Finds progress, man's distinctive mark alone,
> Not God's, and not the beasts': God is, they are,
> Man partly is and wholly hopes to be.

And this progress through struggle is the reason why Rabbi Ben Ezra can advise

> Then, welcome each rebuff
> That turns earth's smoothness rough,
> Each sting that bids nor sit nor stand but go!
> Be our joys three-parts pain!
> Strive, and hold cheap the strain;
> Learn, nor account the pang; dare, never grudge the throe! [10]

So long as pestilence was regarded by the pious as the just visitation of divine wrath, smallpox, yellow fever, and diphtheria swept whole continents unchecked, yet the suffering furnished a stimulus to science which has brought these scourges under control. Man's conquest of nature has been, at every step, a progress through struggle, but there has been progress. The sea, which was such a terror to the ancient Semites, offers a splendid adventure to the modern traveler

[10] Cf. "Browning and the Problem of Evil" by G. Tremaine McDowell, *The Personalist* (July, 1925).

in monster Leviathans gliding swiftly above the waves. Yet
the sea has exacted a heavy toll in human suffering, and to a
Melville, in *Moby Dick*, is still the symbol of the demonic
aspects of nature and the human spirit. D. S. Cairns of Aber-
deen, in a searching analysis of the hostility or indifference
of nature, has shown on evolutionary principles that man's
progress has been organic to nature: "Historically we owe the
very ethical standards by which we condemn nature to the
hard discipline to which she has subjected mankind." [11]

In the realm of social evils, the problem is more involved
and the question of progress perhaps more doubtful. Yet,
as Walter Rauschenbush said, "The idea of solidarity, when
once understood, acts as a theodicy." [12] There are still people
who believe that wars are ordained by God, and perhaps
more who simply believe that they are inevitable in the course
of nature, but the sufferings have become so great that even
victors are losers and men are determined as never before to
find ways for the peaceful adjustment of human affairs.
Whenever economic and political exploitation reduces
people to a sufficient state of poverty and its brood of afflictions, radical reform or revolution is inevitable; that is, in a
free society. In America the concentration of wealth and
social inequality, the wage slavery and periodic unemploy-
ment, have been a scandal throughout this century, but it
has been a period of industrial expansion in which the people
on the whole have been too comfortable to become revolutionaries. What competent observer, especially of the temper
of the people during the great depression of the thirties,
would suppose that Americans will wait so long as Russians
to lay violent hands on the old order?

The social question is whether we can have progress
toward a just society without violent revolution? What

[11] D. S. Cairns, *The Faith That Rebels* (New York: Doubleday, Doran
& Co., 1923), p. 202.
[12] Walter Rauschenbush, *A Theology for the Social Gospel* (New York:
The Macmillan Co., 1918), p. 183.

makes so many despair of progress is that the race does not seem able to treat social problems in the same objective and intelligent fashion as they do disease. History is not very reassuring to the hope that economic and political progress can come by peaceful and orderly adjustment. The most extreme threat, paradoxically, arises from those revolutionaries who believe they can perfect the instruments of dictatorship, in the name of the proletariat, so that they can bring to an end "the dialectic of history" in a classless society. To meet the threat, those who are fearful of their privilege and power oftentimes seem unable to do anything more intelligent than set up machine-gun nests. In spite of all this, it can still be said that poverty and its attendant evils are a constant stimulus to the growth of a higher moral fiber in the social order.

After all, the real danger in the face of evil is not that we shall fail to understand the mystery of a suffering world, but that we shall give up the struggle against it and be sucked down beneath the whirlpool and blotted out like drowning rats in a sewer. It is doubtless a very wise providence which prevents us from finding a final theoretical answer to the problem of evil. Too many of us would bow before the fates and do nothing about it. The fault of many idealistic philosophies, and perhaps all purely metaphysical theodicies, is a certain tendency to narcotize the struggle against evil by some transcendental vision which dims our view of the particular in our comprehension of the Absolute. And the easy explanations which religions have sometimes provided for the evils of the world are a partial justification for the famous Marxian dictum that "religion is the opiate of the people."

Whatever pragmatic value is to be gotten out of the evil in experience depends upon our belief that it can be eliminated, and that it is our constant duty to struggle to that end. A faith which is equal to the extremities of life, and which offers consolation even in defeat, is certainly one of the provisions of religion; but when that aspect cuts the nerve of moral endeavor it ceases to be the faith of the Hebrew-Christian tradition, which as Dr. Cairns so cogently states, is *The Faith That Rebels.*

Chapter 11

HEARSAY AND EXPERIENCE

The somber mood of the Book of Job is not the blackness of despair. There is an undercurrent of hope throughout, even though at times it seems to be a blindfolded hope straining to hear the melody of a single string on life's lyre. The mood is that of a dimly lighted cathedral with a mysterious interplay of changing lights and shadows and above it all a Gothic arch pointing Godward. The high altar is an ash heap before which the anguished soul of Job pours out the bitter complaint of human woe. Richly robed priests come to comfort and remain to castigate. The rolling of distant thunder, like a pedal diapason, sends ecclesiastics scurrying for cover, leaving the sufferer resigned to any fate that may come. Awed by the flash and fury of the elements, he is silenced at first and then fascinated as he hears a rumbling articulation above the organlike thunder. It is the voice of the LORD. The storm subsides and the setting sun casts a mellow glow against the pillars that support the Gothic arch. Job looks up in ecstasy and speaks:

> I had heard of thee by the hearing of the ear,
>> but now my eye sees thee;
> therefore I despise myself,
>> and repent in dust and ashes. (42:5-6)

Thus we come to the final pragmatic suggestion for facing the Job problem: Suffering is a pathway to God, and in a meaningful, personal experience of God the soul finds its balm in Gilead.

A Pathway to God

The experience of Job fulfils the second part of the couplet of Elihu which sets forth the instrumental values which may be found in suffering:

> He delivers the afflicted by their affliction,
>   and opens their ear by adversity. (36:15)

So long as men are prosperous and comfortable, they are likely to be self-sufficient and feel no need of God. That is a peculiarity of human nature. In the time of his affluence, if Job was the typical man of affairs, even though he observed all the forms of piety, he had little time to get acquainted with God. Suffering calls a halt and violently forces on our unwilling attention the consideration of ultimate things. Even that does not always bring man to God. Sometimes the sufferer is repelled. Redemptive suffering must be freely accepted for the possibility it brings of humility and deepening the sense of dependence on God.

Thomas à Kempis, in *The Immitation of Christ*, declares, "It is good that we have sometimes some troubles and crosses; for they often make a man enter into himself, and consider that he is here in banishment, and ought not to place his trust in any worldly thing." Man is a child of nature. Sometimes he glories in that and wants nothing else; that is when he is in health and happiness in this world. If he were an animal only and nothing else, that were enough. But the more he meets the frustrations and tragedy of existence the more he becomes self-conscious and free. Anxiety itself is a function of spirit. He belongs to another world also.

> I am a stranger here;
>   this world is not my home.

Hebrew thought was too deeply grounded on the notion that all suffering is punishment for sin to make great advance toward the conception of a redemptive value in it. This is barely suggested in the Book of Job. Yet in the suffering-servant passage of Isaiah 53, the foundation was laid for New Testament thought on this point. "In the Old Testament," says Albert C. Knudson, "a man might suffer in spite of his being just, but in the New Testament suffering is a necessity for one who is in perfect fellowship with God." [1] The sufferings of Christ in the course of fulfiling his mission brought into the focus of Christian doctrine two elements whose peculiar combination make them unique in religion: one is the idea of a God who suffers, and the other is the picture of a kind of suffering, which, though it may be the very substance of tragedy, is not utterly tragic because it is redemptive. There were suffering gods before Christ but they invoked pity, not worship, primarily. Early Christian thought shows scarcely a trace of pity in reference to Christ's passion. It rather became a symbol of his triumph. "Christian orthodoxy has never sentimentalized the death of its founder," says Shailer Mathews, and he points out that, unique among martyrdoms, the merit of his death became an item in the program of his followers.[2]

For Christians a solution of the Job problem came with two developments of New Testament history, the doctrine of the atonement and the doctrine of divine grace. "God was in Christ reconciling the world to himself, not counting their trespasses against them, and entrusting to us the message of reconciliation" (II Cor. 5:19). The God of Jesus the Christ is not the transcendent Spectator of the Job poem, nor the transcendent Lord or Judge of medieval theology who must maintain dignity and dispense abstract justice. He shares the pain and agony of the human soul through his own self-giving

[1] Albert C. Knudson, *The Doctrine of God* (New York: Abingdon-Cokesbury Press, 1930), pp. 332 ff.
[2] Shailer Mathews, *The Atonement and the Social Process* (New York: The Macmillan Co., 1930), p. 164.

love. "For it was fitting that he, for whom and by whom all things exist, in bringing many sons to glory, should make the pioneer of their salvation perfect through suffering" (Heb. 2:10). God's grace and forgiving love are guaranteed in the love of Christ which was faithful unto death.

In one sense the debate between Job and his friends seems very artificial and unreal. No Christian could ever make such a profession of sinless perfection as Job. In fact, it is strange even to the typical Jewish spirit, as pointed out by the distinguished Jewish philosopher, Paul Weiss, of Yale University: "Job, in his belief that he deserved to prosper, goes counter to the dark, somber, and reasonable temper of most Jews to the effect that men deserve naught but punishment." [3] Biblical thought has stressed rather the sinfulness of human nature, and modern man in general is too much aware of the dark mystery of man's moral struggle. Neither his moral perfection nor his sufferings guarantee man's acceptance with God, but his tribulations bring him to the realization of his need and the sufferings of Christ bring assurance of the grace of God.

The traditional formulations of the atonement doctrine all state the matter as though Jesus paid the whole debt; our sufferings have nothing to do with the reconciliation. Christ's death, conceived as a sacrifice, a ransom, a satisfaction, a substitution, or an example of the results of sin and a moral influence calling us to righteousness, to use all the traditional figures of speech, gives a peculiar significance to the sufferings of Christ but leaves the sufferings of man in general as great an enigma as ever. In the modern world view, struggle and suffering and sacrifice have a cosmic significance which they never had in any of the earlier systems of thought. The formulation of the doctrine of the atonement which adequately interprets the significance of the passion of Christ for our time has not yet been made.

[3] Paul Weiss, "God, Job, and Evil," Commentary (August, 1948).

Christ's sufferings attain their special importance by the fact that they were acquired in the line of duty and were accepted voluntarily in the spirit of unselfish love and are the work of the God-Man. Not all suffering attains such vicarious quality; much of it is the result of selfishness and often it is met with a spirit of revolt. It would seem that adversities best become a pathway to God when we meet them with faith and courage and when they bring us to humility. Yet we do not forget that Job came to his transcendent ecstasy through rebellion.

The solution for Job is in the distinction between hearsay knowledge and personal experience of God, and this is a distinction which strikes the heart of the religious attitude toward all the problems of life. It involves the difference between theory and practice, between rational explanations and personal participation. Religion always begins with a hearsay type of indoctrination, but it is never complete until that is translated into experience.

Hearsay Knowledge of God

What is this hearsay knowledge of God? In a word, it is tradition, the faith of our fathers. None of us has to begin his life where the first man (Mogli, as William McDougall named him) began when he came out of the jungle, nor where Abraham began when he set his face toward the west to go out from the land of his fathers, and the reason is the hearsay knowledge which fathers pass on to their sons. The early part of education must be largely given to learning what the ages have to say to us, and the thorough mastery of some historic period far enough gone to fall into complete perspective is one of the best ways of preparing to meet the problems of today and tomorrow. The human problem is always fundamentally the same, and one's own age is too close to him and he is too deeply involved in it, with his desires, prejudices, and anxieties, ever to understand it or properly to appraise it. The understanding and acceptance of a tradition also provides a sort of interim certainty about fundamental matters while current problems are under investigation. It is quite important to "keep your head when all about are losing theirs," and nothing will achieve that poise more surely than a knowledge of history. Most of the fads and novelties of today are the exploded follies of yesterday. Tradition is crystallized experience; indeed, its very crystallization is its fault. It always takes some of what Walter Lippmann calls the "acids of modernity" to make it sufficiently fluid for progress.[4]

What was the hearsay knowledge in the case of Job? It was the prophetic tradition in Israel (which we have discussed in Chapter 2). The burden of the early prophetic message was that the LORD punishes evil. The nation could not sow the wind and expect to reap zephyrs. The whirlwind was in the offing. Idolatry and priestly graft and exploitation of the poor and foreign alliances would surely be punished. Every calamity that befell the nation was interpreted in the light of this teaching, and by the time of Ezra what had originally been simply a generalized judgment against flagrant sins had been petrified into that complacent orthodoxy of Job's comforters, also reviewed in previous chapters. But to summarize, this was the belief that God is to be understood as abstract justice, rendering to each man measure for measure, evil or good according to the works of the man. It was now much more than a threat against proposed sin; it was a dogma for the interpretation of all suffering. Some of the acids of modernity were needed and they were supplied in such skeptical writings as the Job poem.

There is a very important core of truth in that doctrine. As our world goes most of the time, a man gets about what

4 Walter Lippmann, *Preface to Morals* (New York: The Macmillan Co., 1929), Chap. iv.

is coming to him. If he is faithful and honest and willing to turn his hand and brain to the work of the world, he will gain the respect of his neighbors, he will not lack friends, and he is the more likely to prosper. Morality, diligence, and religion pay. The psalmist no doubt spoke out of long observation of average human experience when he said,

> I have been young, and now am old;
>   yet I have not seen the righteous forsaken
>   or his children begging bread. (Ps. 37:25)

If this expresses humble gratitude to God, or takes adversity as an occasion for self-examination, the sentiment is wholesome. No one goes too far wrong by expecting to reap the fruits of evil-doing or by anticipating pleasure and happiness in well-doing. How different the words sound when the meaning is turned around! when it is taken as a dogma for the judgment of the sufferings of others, or when prosperity is taken as a sign of holiness or the special favor of the Almighty! The notion has been the defense of pious hypocrisy in every age of religion.

The Job problem roots in this misuse of prophetic teaching. The pain of disease was not so intense as the agony of his heart at the thought that if his own experience represented the justice of God, then God is immoral and the world is evil at the core. The skepticism of the book, as most skepticism in the history of philosophy, stems from the stubbornness of daring souls, in the face of powerful hearsay orthodoxy, to insist on the importance of experience. As Ralph Tyler Flewelling puts the matter in a very pointed interpretation of the document, Job is the real man of faith and the friends are the doubters because they find it necessary to lie in order to defend their theory of God.[5] Tradition always solidifies into some sort of rational theory. It is formulated in syllogisms and handed on by coherent argument. The trouble with

[5] Ralph Tyler Flewelling, *Christ and the Dramas of Doubt* (New York: Abingdon-Cokesbury Press, 1933), pp. 78 ff.

such formulations, insisted on as dogma, is that they always run into the equivocal and ambiguous situations of moral man in his struggle upward. This makes necessary the transition from mere theory about God to a personal apprehension.

The necessity of experience to complete the meaning of religion has been the burden of preaching by the rabbis and Christian ministers from the time of Job until today. The file of every preacher of the gospel contains sermons based on two texts from St. John which express the insistence of that writer on the pre-eminence of experience in the knowledge of Christ. One is the word of the blind man after his sight was restored and he was under sharp questioning by the authorities about this Jesus who had restored his sight, "Whether he is a sinner, I do not know; one thing I know, that though I was blind, now I see" (9:25). The other is the challenge of Jesus to Pilate when he had asked him whether he was a king of the Jews, "Do you say this of your own accord, or did others say it to you about me?" (18:34).

Martin Buber, distinguished European rabbi and professor of social philosophy at the Hebrew University in Jerusalem, in the spirit of the Job poets has taught our generation, both Christian and Jewish, a new importance and direction for finding God. The existential situation of modern man makes just as inadequate many of the traditional theological formulations as they were for Job. But we cannot turn to cosmology, as the Semitic poets did, to yield a new and adequate apprehension of God. Buber searches into man's personal experience in the midst of society, to the "I and Thou" relation, to the fellow-feeling and social solidarity which is achieved through conversation and communion (rather than science or the traditional dialectic of philosophy); here he insists that there is a new mystical apprehension of God for our time. Something of the same import comes from those Christian theologians who are finding their central theme in the New Testament agapé (love), notably Nels Ferré. Both insist that the love of God and love for neighbor are inseparable, and that they are apprehended in experience rather than in rational argument. Ferré expounds the matter more from the Biblical and theological point of view; Buber is an incisive critic of man's relation to man. Ferré begins with prayer, Buber with conversation. Both achieve a mystic apprehension of God.[6]

Job keenly feels the inadequacy of the hearsay. Throughout the discourses there is an undercurrent of intense longing for a more intimate contact with God than his normal living had provided, and a rising animation of expectancy. At the end of his second speech (7:21), he anticipates death, but then expects the LORD to grope for him in the dust after he is no more. In his third speech he cries out for a chance to stand in judgment before God with an impartial umpire to arbitrate the difference between them (9:32-33). In the second cycle of speeches, he rises to a height of faith to declare:

> Even now, behold, my witness is in heaven,
>   and he that vouches for me is on high. (16:19).

Then there is the famous disputed passage about the resurrection, in which Job declares, "I know that my Redeemer lives" (19:25). In the last cycle of the debate, when the argument has almost worn itself out, Job gives final utterance to this longing in a passionate outcry:

> Today also my complaint is bitter,
>   his hand is heavy in spite of my groaning.
> Oh, that I knew where I might find him,
>   that I might come even to his seat!
> I would lay my case before him
>   and fill my mouth with arguments.

[6] Compare Nels F. S. Ferré's Evil and the Christian Faith (New York: Harper & Bros., 1947), pp. 139 ff., with Martin Buber's cricitism of Kierkegaard, "The Question to the Single One" in Between Man and Man (New York: The Macmillan Co., 1947), pp. 40-82.

I would learn what he would answer me,
    and understand what he would say to me.
Would he contend with me in the greatness of his power?
    No; he would give heed to me.
There an upright man could reason with him,
    and I should be acquitted for ever by my judge.
Behold, I go forward, but he is not there;
    and backward, but I cannot perceive him;
on the left hand I seek him, but I cannot behold him;
    I turn to the right hand, but I cannot see him. (23:2-9)

Experience of God

We have here no Yoga discipline or purgation of the
Western mystics, but such earnestness and sincerity of a
seeking soul which do not go unrequited. The answer to
Job's longing comes and with overwhelming power. Exhausted by the debate, he settles back upon his ashy bed to
listen with sullen patience to the wordy harangues of Elihu.
A storm is gathering on the horizon and the flash of lightning
outlines the distant sand dunes. One by one the friends make
their exit as the whirlwind comes crashing into the scene.
Job is left alone to the fury of the elements and the despair
and longing of his heart. He bows his head expecting the
stroke of death, but instead is transported into a trance, and
out of the whirlwind he hears the voice of Yahweh.

In the speeches of the LORD, our poet mounts the summit
of poetic power. Many commentators remark to this effect:
that hand and pen have probably never before or since in-
scribed so eloquent a recital of the wonders of creation or the
majesty of the Creator. With the exception of one strophe,
the Voice reviews the marvels of the created world. A series
of questions is propounded, all of which must be answered
with a single negative if answered at all. They are designed
to silence and awe the arrogant spirit of man. The fierce in-
dictments which puny man can bring against him are of little
meaning before the majesty of the Almighty, and yet man

must be dealt with; he cannot be ignored. Surely the Creator and Manager of the universe can be trusted to run its affairs unchallenged by man, who knows but one small corner of the vast domain and that very imperfectly. So far from being able to enter the treasuries of the snow, or to see the treasuries of the hail, or to bind the cluster of the Pleiades or loose the bands of Orion, he does not even know the ways of the wild goats and the wild asses, or the ostrich, or the hawk. He is not the one who giveth the horse his strength.

> Who is this that darkens counsel
>   by words without knowledge?
>
>   *   *   *   *   *
>
> Where were you when I laid the foundation of the earth?
>   Tell me, if you have understanding. (38:2, 4)

He who had been so anxious to set his cause in order before God and fill his mouth with arguments now lies dumb and speechless with awe:

> Behold, I am of small account; what shall I answer?
>   I lay my hand on my mouth.
> I have spoken once, and I will not answer;
>   twice, but I will proceed no further. (40:4-5)

Then the Voice turns from the general providence to the specific charge which Job had made, that the Almighty is indifferent to the just and permits the wicked to prosper.

> Gird up your loins like a man;
>   I will question you, and you declare to me.
> Will you even put me in the wrong?
>   Will you condemn me that you may be justified?
> Have you an arm like God,
>   and can you thunder with a voice like his? (40:7-9)

Job has presumed to stand in judgment on the judgments of God; let him now array himself with majesty and power and see if he can bring the wicked and proud to sudden catastrophe. That would justify his own proud notion that he is wise and powerful enough to save himself (40:10-14).

The final words of the Voice are two long poems descriptive of Behemoth and Leviathan. These are easily identified as hippopotamus and crocodile, two beasts that man has never subdued, and the descriptions of them move with the mystery of the mythical monsters of the primeval struggle out of which worlds came into being. Behemoth is "chief of the ways of God" and Leviathan is "king over all the sons of pride."

Proud man is brought to humble submission:

> I know that thou canst do all things,
>   and that no purpose of thine can be thwarted.
>
> *   *   *   *   *
>
> —now my eye sees thee;
> therefore I despise myself,
>   and repent in dust and ashes.   (42:2, 5-6)

Among the expositors of the Book of Job there are two approaches to this literary manifestation of Deity; one might be called rationalistic and the other mystical. Those who .come through the argument to this climactic point with the notion that there ought to be a rational answer to the problem of evil meet here a dismal disappointment. Some are charmed by the poetry but where is the meaning of it all? And when they observe the collapse of Job in the face of the awaited opportunity to declare his cause, they become scornful. This is not a performance to satisfy either the rationalistic idealist or the humanist. Some stress the critical evidence that these latter sections show the compilation of later poets and editors and dismiss them with scant concern.

Those theists, in particular, who are eager to establish the goodness and providence of God by the evidence of design in nature must look upon this passage with some puzzlement. All the illustrations seem to have been selected because of the fact that they do not exhibit an idealistic purpose. In this they match the contemporary view of nature. The student today, brought up on the struggle-for-survival view of nature, turns with amazement to works which had great influence on the preaching of our forefathers, such as that of William Paley, whose *Natural Theology* was published in 1802. Paley rested his proof of divine goodness on the argument that all the contrivances of nature are beneficial, and that a surplus of pleasure is added to animal sensations. "It is a happy world after all," he says. "The air, the earth, the water teem with delighted existence. In the spring noon, or a summer evening, on whichever side I turn my eyes, myriads of happy beings crowd upon my view."

About the same time Immanuel Kant commented on the LORD's speeches in Job to show the failure of all philosophical attempts to establish a theodicy by the argument from design: "God deigned to disclose the wisdom of his creation to Job on the side of its inscrutableness chiefly." But Kant has a theodicy grounded on faith. To him the devastations of nature support the witness of the practical reason that man "was not born to build everlasting habitations upon this stage of vanity." [7]

Numinous

Two key words in recent theological discussion, applied to these poems of the Voice from the whirlwind, give them a more profound significance. They take us beyond reason into the realm of the mystical. The first is the word *numinous*, which was invented by the German theologian, Rudolf Otto, and expounded in *The Idea of the Holy*.[8] In that work Dr. Otto has given us one of the most important expositions of this section of the Book of Job to be found in current literature. He holds that Chapter 38 "may well rank among the

[7] Quoted from *An Enquiry, Critical and Metaphysical, into the Grounds of the Proof for the Existence of God, and into the Theodicy*, from the translation by John Richardson (London: 1836).

[8] The English translation of *Das Heilige* (1917) was made by John Harvey (New York: Oxford University Press, 1923). The treatment of Job is in Chap. x, pp. 74-84.

most remarkable in the history of religion" because it displays
in rare purity and completeness the numinous quality which
marks the essence of the religious consciousness.

After some thirty years of usage among students of religion, the word still needs exposition. Otto speaks of "a
unique 'numinous' category of value and a definitely 'numinous' state of mind" (p. 7). This means that the word defines
a quality in the object of religious experience and at the same
time it designates the uniquely religious content of experience. It is not to be identified either with the rational or with
the moral. The numinous is the elemental quality which the
Hebrews conveyed in their word qādôsh (holy) before that
word acquired an ethical content. Thus it defines the more
in religious thought and experience which goes beyond reason and beyond moral activity. In content, it is the feeling
of the mysterious, the tremendous, and the fascinating. It
is "primary, unique, underivable from anything else," and is
"the basic factor and the basic impulse underlying the entire
process of religious evolution" (p. 15).

Otto does not believe that the Lord's address in the Book
of Job is intended simply to demonstrate the impossibility of
a theodicy or to induce a mere abject surrender to omnipotence. So strong is the interest in such an interpretation
that we have a tendency to read into the verses some such
notion as that of St. Paul, Romans 9:20: "But, who are you,
a man, to answer back to God? Will what is molded say to
its molder, 'Why have you made me thus?' Has the potter no
right over the clay, to make out of the same lump one vessel
for beauty and another for menial use?" The search for some
rational meaning leads us to want the very words to imply
that God's ways are higher than man's and that there is some
hidden purpose in the mysteries of nature and natural suffering. But no such implication can be found in the poems.
The very choice of poetic figures—the constellations, the
strange and marvelous creatures of the mountains and the

arid land, the Behemoth and the mythical Leviathan—portrays something other than design. They evoke this numinous quality by portrayal of "the downright stupendousness, the well-nigh daemonic and wholly incomprehensible character of the eternal creative power; how, incalculable and 'wholly other,' it mocks at all conceiving but can yet stir the mind to its depths, fascinate and overbrim the heart" (p. 82).

This numinous quality, Otto believes, is a theodicy of its own, better than the one presented by Job's friends and more fundamental than the one generated in Christian history by the rationalist and optimistic tradition. There is something more in it than a mere feeling of mysteriousness. That might strike Job dumb but it could not convict him inwardly. The positive quality of the numinous is the feeling of the august and the resulting fascination. God is justified and Job is brought to peace. All questions about rational purpose are forgotten. Both reconciliation and the desired vindication are achieved without the necessity of reading on to the story of restorations in the epilogue.

Ecstasy

The German-American theologian, Paul Tillich, speaks of the Theophany of Job as an ecstatic experience, and the word *ecstasy* has a significant meaning which illuminates not only this section of the book but the problem as well. There is a similarity to the numinous, although the exposition is different, and Tillich is at pains to emphasize the objective reference in ecstasy and to avoid the danger of reducing the reality to a mere aesthetic or emotional meaning, a danger which inheres in Otto's psychological approach. Tillich is concerned with the being; his approach is ontological.

In ecstasy, the subjective reason is grasped by a mystery of revelation which confronts it from beyond itself. There is a negative kind of ecstasy. "It is the shock subjective reason experiences if it faces its own ground and abyss." And there is a positive ecstasy in which the source of the experience is recognized as revelation or a "ground beyond subject and object." Genuine religious ecstasy cannot be dissolved into mere subjective emotion.

Job certainly goes through both the negative and the positive forms of ecstasy. In every speech of the symposium there is the requisite feeling as he faces the unfathomable mystery of existence and destiny, and there is a postive ecstasy in the final subdued silence which overtakes him, broken only by his protesting gesture and humble confession.

In ecstasy, according to Tillich, reason is not negated but it reaches beyond itself. He also holds that an ecstatic adjustment in the face of evils of existence such as Job achieved, is essential to the idea of divine providence and the establishment of a theodicy. The concept of providence has become questionable simply because it left out this quality and became a rational philosophy. In the ancient world there was a basic conflict between the idea of fate and the notion of providence. It involved the contest between monotheism among the Jews and pagan polythesim. From the prophets to St. Augustine, the great difficulty in trying to establish a theodicy was the effort to justify the notion of divine providence against the deeply ingrained belief of the pagan world in a blind fate. This belief in fate was the ground of the tragic sense of life in Greece which had to be overcome or transcended before a monotheistic faith could be established on a world scale. This was accomplished for the Christian world by two concepts, the Old Testament idea of creation and the New Testament faith that the Christ had overcome fate.

These dogmas established in early Christian theology the concept of divine providence, the faith that God's purposes are ultimately being achieved amid the evils of existence. The paradox of omnipotence and benevolence united as attributes of Deity gradually acquired the status of rationality, and as it did so, not only was the paradox forgotten but the evils faded into an optimistic and idealistic world view. The famous analogy of the mosaic pavement was set forth by St. Augustine.[9] If one examines the pattern closely, the small lines and forms are in confusion. He must stand off and see the whole in proper perspective in order to grasp the meaning and beauty of it all. Augustine, the great philosopher of time, taught Christians the desirability of viewing things under the aspect of eternity (sub specie aeternitatis). Thus the evil becomes a confusion of short lines and shadows fulfiling an essential part of the vast design of God. In the age of reason, Leibnitz thus could maintain that this is the best of all possible worlds, and Paley, the hedonist, could pencil the notes of pain from the struggle for survival into the symphony which his ears heard from birds and bees and beasts. The climax of such optimism, which has brought reaction, was the dialectic interpretation of history in Hegel and Marx. While men have been dreaming of a Utopia which should bring an end to social conflict, the conflict itself has been so vivid in our century that it has brought back the tragic sense of life in a deepening form and with it the pagan doctrine of fate in modern dress.

What Dr. Tillich insists on, in a way which strikes the peculiar need of our time, is that "Christian theology must acknowledge the experience expressed in the idea of fate, and rediscover the paradoxical and ecstatic character of the idea of providence."[10]

[9] De Ordine, which was recently translated under the title "Divine Providence and the Problem of Evil" in The Fathers of the Church: Writings of Saint Augustine (New York: Cima Publishing Co., 1948).

[10] Not all this exposition should be charged to Dr. Tillich, but the quotations are from mimeographed outlines which he provides for his students, and they are quoted by permission. On this topic also see his Systematic Theology (Chicago: University of Chicago Press, 1951), pp. 111-15. Compare his treatment of Otto's thesis, pp. 215-18.

Relevance of Job for Today

These qualities, the feeling of fate and the tragic sense of life, are peculiarly combined in the Book of Job without either the idea of fate or the final tragic despair of the Greeks. The book does not fit easily into the pattern of traditional Christian theodicy. It breathes more the spirit of our age. Our rational attitude today faces the problem of evil with rebellion, as Job did in the symposium. The ecstatic or numinous experiences of religion never meant more than today. They provide that sense of security for values, or consolation in defeat, which lifted Job from his ashy bed, enabled Jesus to set his face resolutely to go up to Jerusalem, and Paul to stand unperturbed and undefeated in the judgment halls of Caesar. We do not have a formal solution of the problem of suffering, but as Albert C. Knudson has said,

> . . . we have something better: we have an attitude of soul, a spiritual experience, by means of which the problem is transcended. It is good to know that our sufferings may be a trial of our faith, a test of our righteousness, that they may in the providence of God be vicarious and redemptive, that they have a disciplinary value, and that they will ultimately give way to a happier future; but it is better still to have a vision of God so rapturous that the sufferings of the present lose their sting, and life is permitted to go on in unruffled peace.[11]

All purely theoretical attempts to explain the meaning of evil by means of a theistic world view, whether metaphysical or theological, run into an insoluble dilemma. God is, by definition, first of all good, and then sufficiently powerful to guarantee the ultimate achievement of his goals. This means, in tradition, the idea of omnipotence, but today we are not so insistent on carrying the matter to the point of absoluteness. If God is powerful enough really to control affairs, then

[11] Albert C. Knudson, *The Religious Teachings of the Old Testament* (New York: Abingdon-Cokesbury Press, 1918), p. 289.

his goodness is in question by the human standard of values because experience has a vast content which to human reason is utterly purposeless and devoid of value. Theoretical solutions either take the form of conceiving some kind of obstruction to the divine good will or they define the divine character in some way which lifts the standard of valuation entirely out of the ordinary meaning of good and evil to human experience. A religious pragmatism and mysticism, however, boldly affirms the paradox and pursues the matter in terms of practical adjustments to evil. Faith in the goodness of God is inspiration for the moral struggle and there is no goodness without this struggle. Omnipotence itself could not create moral value in us, for that depends entirely on our freedom. In the final analysis, there is no goodness but personal goodness and no value except in and for persons; and all goodness, either human or divine, consists in free choices which can be called good. The numinous and ecstatic experiences reinforce the moral struggle, and when the struggle fails on the finite level they provide the confidence in the sureness of the Everlasting Arms. Charles A. Bennett, in one of the most penetrating studies on mysticism in recent times, has this to say: "The mystic alone can read the black book of pessimism to the end, burking none of the world's tragedy and chaos, and still retain the militant address towards evil because he is the conscious ally of that by which the evil may be conquered." [12]

The dilemma confronts man in a preliminary stage, a rationalistic phase of his history, as with Job in the stage of argument. When the ecstatic experience grips him, then the problem is annulled; the rational attributes begin to fade in their application to Deity.

[12] Charles A. Bennett, A Philosophical Study of Mysticism (New Haven: Yale University Press, 1923), p. 162.

INDEX OF SCRIPTURE REFERENCES *

* All quotations are from the *Revised Standard* Version.

215

INDEX OF NAMES AND SUBJECTS